Since time in
Narada and Bh
are synony

Sri Sri Ravishankar
an epitome of joy, love, silence,
humour and deep wisdom,
gives an inspiring discourse on the

Narada Bhakti Sutras

Aphorisms on Love

Narada Bhakti Sutras

His Holiness Sri Sri Ravishankar

First Edition January 2003

Editing, Compiliation & Design : Sharmila Murarka

Acknowledgements : Nalini Semlani, Deborrah Shea, Urmila Devi

Reprint - 2005 (2000 Copies)

The Art of Living

Vyakti Vikas Kendra
19, 39th A Cross
11th Main, 4th 'T' Block
Jayanagar, Bangalore-560 041
Tel : (080) 26645106
Fax : (080) 26635175
Email : vvkpress@bgl.vsnl.net.in

Printed by :
Elegant Printing Works
Basavanagudi, Bangalore - 560 004
Phone : 26615507 Fax : 26677409

Printed in INDIA

Sri Sri Ravishankar

a name that needs no introduction...
beloved of all, man, woman and child -
any country, any religion, any colour, any 'position'.
His love, His wisdom, His Sudarshan Kriya have opened
floodgates within individuals, who themselves are amazed to
find this reservoir of love within themselves -
a deep urge for caring and sharing, building a Divine society,
where peace and love are not words, they exist as reality!

Sadhna, Satsang, Knowledge and Seva -
an amazing amalgamation...life takes on a Divine quality.
At 'Satsangs' with Poojya Sri Sri Ravishankar, one is struck
by the complete simplicity of His profound knowledge
on a kalaeidoscopic range of issues.
The beauty of this knowledge is that it does not remain on the
intellectual level, but is integrated into life.

Narada Bhakti Sutras
is dedicated to Bhakti, (devotion), the culmination of Love.
Here we have a series of talks by the Embodimant of Love,
Sri Sri Ravishankar
given in July 2001, at Lake Tahoe and at Montreal.
Some of the sutras discussed at Lake Tahoe
have been repeated at Montreal.

And because every word spoken by the Master
is so very precious, we bring to you a compiliation of the talks,
as they have been spoken...

Art of Living Publications

Wisdom for the New Millenium
Celebrating Silence
God Loves Fun
An Intimate Note to the Sincere Seeker: Vol. 1-7
Waves of Beauty
Bang on the Door
Hinduism and Christianity
Hinduism and Islam
Time
Heritage of Dalits
Timeless Wisdom
One God, One Truth, One World
The Language of the Heart
Prayer, Call of the Soul
The Way back Home
You are the Sky
Seeds of Wisdom

*The teachings of SRI SRI RAVISHANKAR
are available in the form of books, video recordings and audio
tapes in more than 100 countries worldwide,
as well as every city in India.*

*For further information :
Tel : 641-472-9892 Fax : 641-472-0671
Email : bookstore@artofliving.org
Website : www.bookstore.artofliving.org*

CONTENTS

Love is not an act -
it is a result

Love does not give rise to more questions -
it is the answer for all questions

Love is not a path -
it brings you back home

Love   IS   Home

A Bridge to the Divine

Athato bhaktim vyakhya syamah

Sa tvasmin param prem rupa

Amrit swarupa cha

*Yallabhadhva puman siddho bhavati, amrito
bhavati, tripto bhavati*

*Yatprapya na kinchid vanchati,
na shochati, na dweshti, na ramate,
notsahi bhavati*

Yadgyatva matto bhavati, stabdho bhavati,

atmaraamo bhavati

Sa na kamayamana, nirodha rupatvat

Nirodhastu loka veda vyapaara nyasah

Tasmin ananyata tad virodhishu udaseenta cha

Anyashrayanam tyagah ananyata

*Loka vedeshu tadanukul acharanam
tadvirodhishudasinta*

Om Namoh Bhagavate Vasudevaya
Om Namoh Bhagavate Vasudevaya
Om Namoh Bhagavate Vasudevaya

Life springs from love - the origin is love and life seeks love. The goal of life is also love and, in between, life is sustained by love. There is not a single creature or living entity on this planet that has not known love or is devoid of love. Yet, love in its many distortions has brought so much misery in life.

Love is known as three different flavours
· of affection
· love towards companion and
· respect - appreciation

If we are made up of a substance called love, then why don't we experience it? Why is there so much misery? If love is everywhere in creation, why is there a seeking for love? Why do we seek love? When these questions start bothering the human mind, then one's spiritual journey has begun. What is love? The Rishi Narada brought out these *Bhakti Sutras - aphorisms on love.*

In the first *Sutra* he says :

Athato - *Now*, let me enunciate what is *'Bhakti'*, what is devotion.

Athato bhaktim vyakhyasyamah

What is that love which is devoid of imperfection? What is that

1

love which crowns all other love? What is that love which contains all other love? Such love, such a pinnacle of love, is called devotion and I will enunciate it. What is that love? The most difficult thing to do is to describe feelings - any feeling for that matter. It is not easy to put feelings into words or to make someone understand intellectually what the feeling is. It is a humungous task.

Narada ventured - as only Narada can venture. One who has lived that devotion alone can venture into describing it. In the first Sutra Narada says, *Athato* - "Now let me enunciate what is love." One who has not been a seeker, one who has not understood life in its various facets, cannot grasp what Narada is saying First that urge has to come - *"I want to know a love that is free from misery, free from attachment, free from entanglement, free from all sorts of hooks."* When that deep urge has begun, then the Master, the Rishi, the Muni can speak - can say words, which go directly into the heart of the person. For such a seeker, Narada says, "Now let me enunciate *Bhakti*, devotion."

The word, *'Narada'* itself is so beautiful. It is the spoke that joins the circumference to the centre. One who holds you towards the centre is Narada. Often love makes you uncentred, it throws you off-balance, it makes you emotionally and physically weak. Though love is the greatest strength on this planet, without wisdom, the same love makes you weak, absolutely weak, isn't it so? Narada - one who holds you to the centre, yet makes your life rise to the pinnacle of love. He says :

Sa tvasmin param prem rupa

Devotion is ultimate love, the pinnacle of love in *Him*, in *That*. Often love turns into hatred, anger, sour feelings. But the love to the Divinity does not. The next Sutra goes :

Amrit swarupa cha

It is immortal, undying, because it is unconditional - it is not attached to some strings. When you love somebody, you don't care what they do with you, how they behave with you. You simply love them. Even in the case of the child and the mother, you have had many such examples where the children are not so kind, but the mother is always kind.

You know, I heard about an instance in a train at a railway station, where a son had an argument with the mother, an elderly lady, and he really beat her up. She was all bruised, but when the police came to catch the son, she said, "No no, don't do anything to my son." She prevents the police from taking action on her son, who has been very brutal. Getting angry she says, "Never mind, he's my son." The police is trying to discipline her son, but she doesn't want that to happen.

Love is unconditional. Such unconditional love is *amrit swarupa* - undying, immortal, it makes you immortal. It is not that one day you fall in love and the next day you fall out of love. Devotion is not that. It stays deep inside, even if you don't feel it everyday on a day-to-day basis. Often people feel devotion one day and they start repeating all those exercises so that they can feel it again, but it doesn't happen. But it remains, it is undying. Once someone tastes the pinnacle of love, they can never forget it, they can never leave it. So that love is undying.

Yallabdhva puman siddho bhavati,
amrito bhavati, tripto bhavati

Having attained that, human life becomes perfect. There is nothing that you feel you don't have. That perfection dawns in life. *Siddho bhavati, amrito bhavati* - you recognise that something deep inside which has never aged, never dies. *Tripto bhavati* - it brings such fulfilment. Love brings such fulfilment in life.

Yat prapya na kinchid vanchati, na shochati,

na dweshti, na ramate notsahi bhavati

Having attained that, there is no more craving, no more desires. *Na shochati* - you will not sit and cry for anything, there is no sadness. *Na dweshti* - you do not hate anything. *Na ramate* - nothing else is 'rejoiceful'. Nothing else is pulling you off your centre, nothing else is charming. *Notsahi bhavati* - then there is no other enthusiasm or excitement that can take you off. That does not mean you are devoid of enthusiasm - *notsahi bhavati*. You are not over-enthusiastic, not over-excited about anything.

Yat gyatva matto bhavati, stabdho bhavati, atmaramo bhavati

Matto bhavati - knowing which you become intoxicated; *stabdho bhavati* - so still deep within you. *Atmaramo bhavati* - you are reposing in the Self. Only love can make you repose in the Self, only love can quieten you; *matto bhavati* - only love can intoxicate you. There are so many types of intoxication, but the intoxication that comes out of love is *the* intoxication, the *supershot*. You are amazed, wonder-struck. It is baffling. *Atmaramo bhavati* - and it reposes you in the Being.

The Rishi addresses all the three levels. Emotionally you get intoxicated, intellectually you are wonder-struck and you repose in the Self. The three layers of our existence are the Spirit (the Self), the Mind (the Intellect) and the Emotions. How does love have such a profound impact on all three layers? Cravings, desires and aversions arise in the heart. Curiosity, inquisitiveness, enquiry are in the intellect. Joy comes out of intoxication. That is why many people get into intoxication or curiosity when they read all sorts of magazines or watch television. Everything is for the intellect - to calm it down and satisfy the urge of the intellect to know. There is nothing so wonderful, so awesome, as this deep devotion.

Stabdho bhavati, atmaramo bhavati - is this just an emotional exercise or will it take us further towards the ultimate reality, the truth to Self-realisation? The Rishi says, "It takes you to the Self. Such is

4

the glory of Bhakti, of love."

Om Namoh Bhagavate Vasudevaya
Om Namoh Bhagavate Vasudevaya
Om Namoh Bhagavate Vasudevaya

Yat gyatva matto bhavati, stabdho bhavati, atmaramo bhavati

Knowing which you become intoxicated, spellbound and you repose in the Self. There is nothing that can intoxicate you like love. And all the intoxication that people use is to be in that love, is in the search for that love. But they are searching for love in the wrong place. It is the frustration, the 'unfulfilment' that makes one go for intoxicants, isn't it so? What happens when you are intoxicated? The 'two' disappears, the 'other' vanishes. When the other vanishes, then you are more at ease and love is that which gives you such ease, such comfort.

Divine love intoxicates you. Just knowing Divine love, you get intoxicated, spellbound and wonder-struck. When we are miserable, we ask many questions, " Why this, Why this?" When the questions turn into wonder, love arises. Love does not give rise to more questions - it is the answer for all the questions.

Love is not a path actually. Love is home. Love brings you back home. Love is not an act or an action. It is a result.

Then the next question arises, "How can I have it? That's what

5

I want. Yes. What you are saying is right! How can I have it? I want to have it. I desire for it." Then the Rishi says :

Sa na kamayamana, nirodha rupatvat

It cannot be an object of desire. When the desires cease, then love can be felt, experienced. Don't make love an object of desire. Desire means what? Not now, not this; something in the future. Desire simply means, 'not *now*, not *this* - *that* and *then*'. Desire causes such feverishness, love is such a cooling impact. *Sa na kamayamana* - don't make love an object of desire, the goal of your desire. When the desires calm down, you realise that love is right here - Now. That is why Buddha said that desires are the cause of sorrow and misery. Love is the goal of all desires and when you cannot have, when you cannot experience or achieve that love, then hatred and anger come. The desire for love brings all other imperfections, for e.g. frustration. Whether fulfilled or unfulfilled, desire brings frustration. This is the nature of desire. Love cannot be achieved by just desiring it because it is the cessation of desire. It is the source or goal of all desires - *sa na kamayamana*.

Then what is that cessation? How does one stop that?

Nirodhastu loka veda vyapara nyasah

It is taking a break from all activities, whether worldly or spiritual, whether religious or material - being centred in both activities. *Nirodhastu* - there is a feverishness to do something, to achieve something. You say, "I don't want anything material," but then it could switch over to wanting to achieve some heaven, some spiritual merit, or bliss or some state of consciousness. See, you are still holding on to the desire and the action, but it has shifted from the material to the more ethereal, non-material. Our mind is so tricky.

6

Loka veda vyapara nyasah - you cannot leave activity just like that. So what can you do? If you are 100% in an activity, then you become free from the activity. You are able to rest from that activity. This is what we don't do. Being 100% in an activity *centres* you. Desire is not being involved 100% in action. Suppose you want to drive and go to Los Angeles - you just drive and go; but if you just sit and keep thinking about it, it creates the feverishness. This is desire. Desire is chewing on to something and not swallowing it - not really acting on it. Those activities which you have to do, do them and rest. Those which you don't need to do, leave them and rest.

Nyasah - being centred, letting go. However important an activity is, are you able to let go of it in a moment? Then you will see that it does not bother your mind, it does not bother you and it increases your efficiency. It is your attachment to an activity that makes that activity suffer, whether it is spiritual or material. Your obsession to act, your inability to retire and repose in the Self brings you frustration. Do anything with 100% and you will be able to drop it effortlessly. This ability to *let go* comes to you. Often you let go of things when you are frustrated. When you can drop and quit in a moment, without getting frustrated, then Yoga happens - you have retired back to the Self. You are holding onto things, onto activities and that holding on creates frustration. This is what desire does.

Desire is trying to hold on to air in a fist. How much air can you hold in the fist? The more you tighten your grip, the lesser air you can hold. Love is like the vast sky and the sky cannot be held in the fist. You have to open your palm. That is *nirodha* - when you open your palm, the entire sky is in there and if you hold a mirror in your hand, you can have the sun, the moon - everything. A small palm can hold the sun, but not the fist - *nirodha rupatvat*.

Nirodhastu loka veda vyapara nyasah - being centred, being

100% in activity and rest. This is the way to be in Divine love.

Tasmin ananyata tad virodhishu udasinta cha

Often love is thought to be between two - one and the other. When there is another, you don't feel totally one with the person. You always question and doubt the other person's love for you. If you doubt whether the other person really loves you or not, you will be unable to love them unconditionally, unable to merge with them. Certain things you have to take for granted. One thing is the love of the other person from whom you want love. You have to take it for granted. Even if the love is not there, you must feel that it is there.

Tasmin ananyata - means feeling totally one with the other. That is Divine love. Be indifferent to anything that appears to be opposing it. It might happen that you are in love with God, and sometimes things happen that don't seem to show that God is really in love with you. But ignore those things. A saint was once spreading the message of God in villages. One rainy day he came back home and found that most of the roof of his little hut lay broken in the rain. His disciple got very angry and blamed God for being so cruel. "We have been working so hard for you and you couldn't even save one roof for us!" he complained. On the other hand, the saint was so thankful, "Oh God, you are so kind, you saved half the hut so that our heads don't get wet. In this big storm the whole house could have been destroyed. Now we can also see the stars and the moon."

Tasmin ananyata tadvirodheshu udasinta cha - whatever appears to be opposing love, you just be indifferent to it. Otherwise it is very easy to get drawn into the opposite values of love, hatred, anger, jealousy and frustration.

If you want to be centred in love, you have to drop anything that appears to be opposing love, otherwise you will be caught up in the cycle of opposites and you will never be free, you can never achieve that perfection. You are born to be perfect - *siddho bhavati* and the perfection is not in action or speech, perfection is in the Being. The perfection in the Being alone can bring perfection in speech and action; and to be perfect in the Being, you need to immerse yourself in that intense love. What is *ananyata bhakti*? How does one feel this sense of 'no other'?

Anyashrayanam tyago ananyata

Often you have so many other supports, for e.g. you are on a spiritual path and you go to an astrologer and ask if you will make progress? What will happen? You are taking another support. Letting go of all the supports is *anyashrayanam.*

Niradhar - that is dropping the crutches - and the mind is looking for crutches. It is looking for some anchor here and there, for e.g., if you feel negative, you go and talk to someone. If anyone supports your negativity, you start feeling better. If someone shuns your negative statement, it irritates you.

Anyashrayanam tyago ananyata - letting go of all supports. Krishna said in the Bhagavad Gita: *ananyaas chinteyeh janha paripaas* - I am there for the one who is one-pointed and does not look for other supports. "I become the feet for those who do not look for crutches, I become the eyes for those who do not look for glasses."

Loka vedeshu tadanukul aacharanam tadvirodheshu udaseenta

In the world, as well as in spiritual matters, act towards that which nourishes this love, accept that which moves you in the direction of this love and be indifferent to that which is not supporting this love, because life is full of opposites. In life both things, events will

9

happen - those that will support your hatred and destroy love, and those that will destroy hatred and support love, because the field of activity and life is full of opposite values. The same occurs in the scriptures, too - one scripture will authenticate this and another will authenticate that and if you go into all this, you may get really confused. Even in the name of *Dharma* - righteousness, people can make a lot of mistakes. If Jesus was crucified, he was crucified since it was thought that he had been blasphemous - that he had committed a blasphemy against God.

Loka vedeshu tadanukul acharanam tadvirodheshu udasinta - if the activities in the world become an obstruction for your growth, then act skilfully. Often people prepare for *Pujas* or ceremonies, but the preparations eat up all their time. So when they actually sit for meditation, *Puja* (prayers), their minds are all over, caught up in insignificant little things. All the preparations have been in vain. Your aim is to sit and meditate, but you are upset because someone next to you is snoring. So the whole exercise has become futile. You then sit in an angry mood and cannot meditate. So when opposites come your way, take it with ease. Be indifferent. If you are sitting for meditation and someone is irritating you, take it lightly. Otherwise, there is no point in sitting with your eyes closed, getting irritated. Just be indifferent to anything that seems to be opposing it.

If you can be in love, be in love. If you cannot be in love, at least be indifferent. Don't swing to the opposite of love, that is hatred. You cannot force your self to love something that you don't like, but you can definitely be indifferent to it. Don't force yourself to love things which you cannot. Just be indifferent and wait. It is a great secret - indifference. But you know, indifference will irritate people more than hatred! If you hate somebody, they are at ease, but if you are indifferent, they will feel uncomfortable. To anything that appears to be a conflict, indifference is the solution. Conflict has never brought joy. Even in the time of the *Ramayana*, Rama fought the war and there was no joy later, only misery. Same with *Mahabharata* - after the war there was no joy.

Conflicts cannot bring peace.
Whether solved or resolved - there is no question of peace.
With indifference, there is hope.

Loka vedeshu tadanukul acharanam - behave in such a manner that it is supporting to love and be indifferent to anything that appears to be opposing love. Again, love is not just an emotion, it is not being mushy-mushy. Love is the innermost strength, love is the force that you are. We depend so much on the expression of love. This is not *ananya bhakti*. If you are dependent on an expression or a gesture from someone, to feel love for them, I tell you that you are mistaken and you have not grown. If you can see love beyond expressions, beyond the physical gestures, if you can peep into the Being, you can see that there is no other - there is no difference, there is only absolute oneness. That is *ananyata*. Like when the child is sometimes cranky, rebellious, the mother sees beyond the expression. That 'connectedness' of you with the Divinity, with the whole world, with the creation makes you perfect, makes you stable, makes you intoxicated, makes you fulfilled. Otherwise you go with a lack consciousness, with a craving - "I want, I want." The Rishi says, *sa na kamyamana* - it is not a subject of craving, it is Being.

11

Beginning the Spiritual Journey

Athato bhaktim vyakhya syamah

Sa tvasmin param prem rupa

Amrit swaroopa cha

Yallabhadva pooman siddho bhavati, amrito bhavati, tripto bhavati

Yat prapya na kinchad vanchati,
na shochati, na dweshti, na ramte,
notsaahi bhavati

Yat gyaatva matto bhavati, stabdho bhavati,
aatmaraamo bhavati

Sa na kamayamaana, nirodha roopatvat

Nirodhastu loka veda vyapaara nyasah

Om Namoh Bhagavate Vasudevaya
Om Namoh Bhagavate Vasudevaya
Om Namoh Bhagavate Vasudevaya

If you ask yourself a straight question, "What is it that you want in your life?" It will boil down to one thing and that is love. Behind every desire there is love, isn't it? Yet, life cannot move an inch without love; life has sprung from love, moves in love, and its culmination is also love.

Yet we see that life is full of problems. Sometimes if there is no love, then life seems to be better because then there are no problems. Love comes with this tail called problems. If you love objects more, then that becomes greed. If you love people more, it is entanglement. If you love yourself too much, that is ego-centrism, arrogance. If you love someone too much, then jealousy comes behind that. Whether jealousy, greed, lust or anger, there is love present underneath.

Love, when it ferments, becomes hatred.
Love, when it gets distorted, becomes fear.

It is love that causes fear. It is love that is the cause for anger. You love perfection, so you are angry at imperfection. Suppose you don't love perfection, there is no question of being angry. Just search underneath your anger, there is love. Every problem on this planet is caused by love. So, many people prefer not to love, they shut off...cut themselves off. Some run away from society, some remain in an indifferent state, like a log of wood, almost dead.

But this is not life, isn't it so? Then what is the purpose in life? What is the goal in life? What do you want in life?

He says the search in life is for a love that is free from all these distortions, all these negative emotions.

Love often suffocates you, but you cannot have love without freedom. Like the spider, you know, it makes its own web and it gets trapped in its own web. Yet the spider cannot be there without the web, then it is no spider at all.

Human life is in a similar situation. It cannot be without love. Like the spider weaves its web from it's own saliva, we weave our world with our own love and we get trapped in our own world. Love suffocates you. It makes you obliged, it takes away your freedom. But the innate tendency of human life is to be free. You want to enjoy freedom. So the quest, the search, is for such a love that does not take away your freedom. Infact, the love that establishes you away from the imperfections of jealousy, greed, anger, and upholds you in its pure essence, that love is called devotion. That is called *bhakti*. That is called love, the *Divine love*.

How do you get it? Who has really got that love? Who has lived that? This is the beginning point of the spiritual journey. The spiritual journey is not a fantasy of attaining something different. It is the fulfillment of life's ultimate aim or goal, which is bhakti, the Divine love. It is also called devotion. In Sanskrit *bhakti* itself means that which is common between you and the infinite space. That which is there in you, as well as in the Divine; that which you share with the Divine, that which shines *is* bhakti.

If you do not know love at all, you cannot understand it at all. You have to know love, and when you know love, then you can understand what bhakti is. And there is not one creature on this planet that doesn't know what love is.

13

So how do you get to the goal? One needs to go to a saint, and one such saint was Narada. In ancient times Narada was known to be a troublemaker. The name Narada means he is here, he is there also, he is on both sides. He is with this party, he is with the other party, also. He says something here, something there also and bridges them both. Even today in India, if someone is playing both sides you say "Oh you are like Narada." You are here, you are there, you are everywhere. But he always ends up doing good for both parties. That was the skill of Narada. It means that two parties, which appear to be completely opposite, are both comfortable with Narada. And he somehow bridges them both. In the Puranas there are ample number of stories about Narada and his mischief. *Nara-da*, the word itself means "the one who joins the centre and the circumference, who is the spoke."

See, when you are in love, you are not centred, you are out there. You are so spaced out. When you are centred, you don't seem to be so light and joyful. You are very serious. But Narada makes you different. He makes you centred and, at the same time, makes you light and expanded. A centre without a circumference is no centre at all. What is it centre of? And a circumference without a centre simply cannot exist. Yet, though they are so apart, Narada bridges them both. He makes love so practical in life, yet love is the most abstract thing in this universe. There is nothing as abstract as love, yet there is nothing as concrete as love.

And Narada makes it evident. He wrote these eighty-four sutras which came to be known as the *Bhakti Sutras,* the *Aphorisms on Love.*

The first sutra begins :

Athato bhaktim vyakhya syamah

" I will explain what is devotion, the true love, Divine love is."

14

Athato and then now, he starts. When now? After what? After you have searched for love here there, here there and you are tired. And also after you have known what love is, then I can tell you about Divine love.

Love has many manifestations such as affection that you have for those who are younger than you. With children you have affection. With those who are of your age, you have friendship. With those elder to you, you have respect, honour. Similarly, you have love for objects, love for animals, love for trees, love for food and music, love for people and love for yourself. To some extent you may know all this. Your likes and dislikes are also based on love. When you become even a little bit aware of these tendencies in your life and there is a quest for something higher, the ultimate goal of your life, then Narada comes into the picture.

A Master cannot give to you unless you want it.

So that desire, that innate desire in you to *want* to know, is the seed that can sprout further.

Sa tvasmin param premrupa - now I will enunciate what Divine love is. A person who cannot see, cannot be shown what light is. A person who cannot hear, cannot be made to understand what sound is. You can only make one understand with what one already knows. Some may not be able to see, some may not be able to hear, but everyone can feel love. That is why he starts *Athato* 'and then now'. Even stones can feel love. Trees can feel love. Dogs can feel love. Animals can feel love. You know cats, if you really love cats, they come near you and they purr. Dogs express their love. They run around you wagging their tail. They jump all over the place. If you are away for a couple of days and come home they go mad, they go crazy. Just looking at you they don't know what to do. They run all over you.

You cannot miss love in your life. You know something about love, so whatever you know, from then on we will begin. He says *Athato* - now, and then now let us ponder over what is devotion, what is bhakti. In the next sutra he says - *amrit swarupa cha.*

This is one form of ultimate love. Ultimate love in him or in that. *Param premrupa* - often you hate the person with whom you are in love. And you are afraid of the person with whom you are in love. You are jealous of the person with whom you are in love. And anger is also triggered very fast. But to be free from this, the ultimate love is *amrit swarup cha.* The second sutra says that it is non-changing, it is immortal. The love that does not die. It's easy to fall in love and fall out of love. One day you fall in love and a couple of months later you seem to fall out of love. But the Divine love, here, now, we are talking about the goal, is *amrit swarup cha* - it can never change, it is undying, it is unconditional.

In ancient days the saints used to first enunciate the goal, and then used to say the means of it, how to get it. You should have the final address and then the map on how to get to the final address. So to begin with he is saying , "What is that ultimate love, what can you figure about it, the ultimate love, the bhakti which doesn't die." However you want to get out of it, you cannot. However you want to get rid of it, you cannot - because it is undying. It is non-changing. These are the characteristics of that ultimate love for which there is such a deep longing in you, a deep urge in you. That love is undying.

A story about Mullah Nasiruddin. He was in love with a girl but he married somebody else. Someone asked, "I thought you were in love with someone else?" "Yes", said Mullah, "I don't what to marry her because then my love will disappear. So I keep loving her but I married somebody else."

We fall in love and we fall out of love because we do not know what is the ultimate love, what is Bhakti. The totality of love, knowing which you become *amrit swarupa cha* - means that it is immortal, non-changing, it can never die, undying love. Y*allabdhva puman siddho bhavati* - having attained that love, one becomes perfect. If you are striving for perfection, the way to attain it is the totality of love. Attaining bhakti alone makes you perfect. *Siddho bhavati* - Siddha means perfected being; your Being becomes perfect.

There are three levels of perfection. Perfection in action, perfection in your speech and perfection in your Being, in your mind. Some may do their actions perfectly, but their feelings and their words may not be so perfect. Some have good feelings, but their actions are not perfect. In tropical countries you find that people feel very good, they speak very nicely, but when it comes to action it doesn't get done. In cold climate countries, people's actions get done but inside they are very rigid, stiff, sometimes angry and upset. But Siddha is one who is perfect in the feeling, in speech and in action.

You can never be 100% accurate in the action, but you can be 100% accurate in the Being, in the state of Being - that is called *siddho bhavati. Yallabdhva puman siddho bhavati* - and love alone can bring you such perfection. You become so perfect, so complete, because there is no more craving, there is nothing more to achieve. You are not journeying anywhere. You are at home. *Amrito bhavti* - he becomes immortal. He knows this consciousness, this Being, is not just the body or the mind. It is eternal and immortal. *Tripto bhavati* - so fulfilled. Fulfillment is one of the signs of Divine love. If someone is not fulfilled and is frustrated, you cannot say this person has attained Divine love.

In the next sutra he says:

**Yad prapya na kinchid vanchati na shochati,
na dveshti, na ramate notsahi bhavati**

Having attained which, there is no desire left.
Na shochati - nothing to grieve about.
Na dweshti - nothing to hate, nothing to be so excited about.
Notsahi bhavati - nothing to be motivated about.

You know for every action there is a motivation behind that action. Something motivates you because you are going to get something out of it. But one who has attained love has no other motivation at all. Whatever you desire, the ultimate goal of all desires is to be in love. When that is already there, what is there to desire? One of the signs of Siddhi is you have things even before you feel the need for them. Before you feel thirsty, there is plenty of water. And before you feel hungry, people are already offering you food to eat. Even before desires arise, they are already fulfilled, so where is the question of galloping on a desire?

We are not even aware where our desires are taking us. We are galloping on such a horse of desire, without awareness, without knowing where we want to go, what we want to do. *Na kinchid vanchati* - no desires are left to be fulfilled. In a devotee's heart, as soon as a desire arises, it already gets fulfilled. Nature awaits to fulfil the needs of one who is in deep love with the entire existence.

Buddha has said desire is the cause of misery, of sorrow. When there is no desire arising, where is the question of sorrow? There is nothing to be grieved about. *Na, dveshti* - hatred comes behind the grievances. They are all linked, do you see that? You have a desire and when that doesn't get fulfilled, you become upset, sad and when you are sad, you don't want to be in a sad state, so you start hating that person, or that object, or that thing. Hatred is behind the sorrow or the pain. A relationship causes pain and pain is not palatable to any living creature. So one starts hating the source of pain, not knowing it is one's own mind. We project that on to the other person, other object, other thing. So then there is no question of hating anybody here. *Na dveshti, na ramate notsahi bhavati* - nothing to be motivated, nothing to be excited about.

Is it a very dull state then? There is no excitement, there is no hatred. Is it so? It does not mean you are devoid of enthusiasm, that you are not enthusiastic about anything or that you are not excited about anything

In the next sutra he says:

Yad gyatva, matto bhavati

Knowing which one is intoxicated! When you go through all this paraphernalia of negative emotions, that is when you just want to forget everything. Then people just want to drink and intoxicate themselves. But love is the best intoxicant available. Divine love is such an intoxication. *Yat gyatva, matto bhavati* - knowing which you become drunk, you get intoxicated, spaced out.

Stabdho bhavati - what else will any of this excitement do to you? It brings you to a state of amazement, doesn't it? "Ahh, wow!" This feeling arises in you. Love takes you to that state. Knowing which you become so stunned, smitten, completely awestruck! *Atmaramo bhavati* - you become so still, you repose in yourself. You are in such deep rest, deep peace. You are rejoicing yourself and - *atmoramo bhavati* - reposing in the Self.

All these are the glories of love. "How can I have it now? I just want to have that, nothing more, finished with everything else - no job, no work. I will leave everything, I want just that. How can I have it....?"

This desire to have such an ultimate love, which has been painted into such a glorious picture, this feverishness if it arises in you, then Narada is there waiting with a stick, right in front of you. He says:

Sa na kamyamana, nirodha rupatvat

It is not an object of desire, stop wanting it. You know, when you want to sit for meditation, the more you want that thoughts should not come, the more they come. The mind works on a completely different set of laws. Sometimes people say, "I want nothing, I just want liberation." This desire for liberation or desire for the ultimate sometimes makes them go around in circles. When it comes to knowledge, you must have a little desire for liberation to be free. But when it comes to Divine love, he says it is not an object of desire.

Love is not an object of desire. Love is what you are. So *nirodha rupatvaptvat* - settle down, calm down, quiet down. It is like you are wanting to rest, but you keep running from room to room, "Oh, I want to sleep. I want to sleep." All that you want is to relax, but you are running. How can you relax if you are running? If you can relax here, you can relax there also. If you can relax in your living room, you can relax in your bedroom. If you cannot relax in your bedroom, running around the house cannot bring you relaxation. Whether it is on the street or under a tree in the park or home or on the bus, anywhere, wherever you are, you can relax. Isn't that so?

When you want to swim in the lake, you can jump from any side of the lake. Even if you take a boat and jump from the middle of the lake, it is the same as jumping from the shore. You cannot learn swimming unless you are in the water. You cannot say you will first learn swimming and then get into the water. "I don't want to wet my feet, my socks will get wet, but I want to swim." This is not possible. *Sa na kamyamana* - it is not an object of desire, you cannot make it into an object of desire. *Nirodha rupatvat* - it is of the nature of restraint, of relaxation, of retiring.

If one is in a corridor and is walking from this end to that end, and all the person really wants is to relax, what you will say? "Wherever you are, just sit and relax. That is called *nirodha* - withdraw. No, withdraw is not the correct word, retire, repose. Repose wherever you are - *nirodha rupatvat*.

Nirodhastu loka veda vyapar nyasah

What are you retiring from? From all worldly and religious activities. You do worldly activities in order to gain comfort and religious activities in order to gain some spiritual merit. You do so many charities and work so that when you die and go to heaven, there you will enjoy these comforts. There is this desire to gain a better accommodation in heaven, to have a more comfortable air conditioned room if you have earned the merits (laughter)!

A gentleman came to me and said, "Guruji, my mother wants to see you. She wants to ask a question." When she met with me, she said, "See, I am going to die in a few months or maybe a few years, but I am not used to new places. How is it there in the heavens? I think you know how it is there. Can you tell me what I should do to prepare myself? You see, I don't get any sleep when I change places. When I go to New York from Connecticut, I cannot sleep. So I am a little anxious to know how it is there, on the other side." I told her; "Don't worry mother, all will be very comfortable. You will sleep well there also. You better sleep here. Thinking about sleeping there, don't lose your sleep here." She kept saying, "I'm not used to new places you know..." (laughter)

Relax from both worldly and religious activities. Retire from all activities. Sometimes people retire easily from worldly activities but they go on doing other things non-stop - using rosaries non-stop, chanting non-stop, doing something. And this non-stop doing wears you out. You feel worn out and tired and all that you do is fall asleep. *Loka veda vyapar nyasah* - retiring from both spiritual and secular activities, religious and social activities. In any activity maintaining

21

that calm.

Another meaning for *nyasah* is not acting out of feverishness.

How can you retire? Does that mean not doing anything at all? Just sit? Do neither worldly activity nor spiritual activity? No. When can you really retire? When you are really into the activity. Only then does retirement really mean anything. If you never got a job, there is no question of retirement. An unemployed person cannot retire. Only one who is in some employment can retire. So when can you retire? When you are engaged in an activity, then you can retire. So moderate activity is essential.

This word *nyasah* also means being centred. Being centred in any activity you do - spiritual, social or religious. Be centred, maintain that calm, maintain that balance. Being centred in all activities and in your work - not to act out of feverishness.

Rejoice without Conflict

Bhavatu nischaya dadhyardurdhvam shastra rakshanam

Anyatha patitya shankaya

Lokopi tavdeva bhojanadi vyapara stvasharira dharanavadhi

Tallakshannani vachyante nana matbhedat

Poojadishu anurag iti parasharyah

Kathadishviti Gargah

Atmarati avirodhena iti Shandilyah

Naradastu tadarpita akhilacharata tadvismarne param vyakulteti

Astya evam evam

Yatha vraj gopikanam

Tatrapi na mahatmya gyana vismrityapavadah

Tadviheenam jaarannamiva

Nastyeva tasmin tatsukh sukhitvam

Kathadishviti Gargah

Atmarati avirodhena iti Shandilyah

Naradastu tadarpita akhilacharata tad vismarne param vyakulteti

Yatha vraj gopikanam

Sa tu karma gyana yogebhyah api adhiktara

Om Namoh Bhagavate Vasudevaya
Om Namoh Bhagavate Vasudevaya
Om Namoh Bhagavate Vasudevaya

Love can only blossom in freedom. When freedom is restricted, love suffocates. You need to be free. Often love stifles.When you are in love or when you love somebody, you feel stifled because you are obliged. When there are so many obligations that you need to fulfil, then these obligations become like a load on your head and you get the added responsibility not to hurt the people you love and who love you. In a subtle sense, this takes the freedom away and slowly demands start arising in you. The moment demand arises in you, know that love is on its death-bed. Love is in an oxygen chamber and it doesn't live very long.

Demand destroys love. Freedom is essential.

So whether in the world, in religious or in spiritual matters, follow love rather than the rules. This was the sutra that we heard.

A lover is beyond all rules. There is no rule on how to express your love. All expressions are a spontaneous outburst of love and love finds its own expressions - you cannot streamline it. Your eyes cannot hide the love, your gestures cannot hide the love, your steps cannot hide the love. Love flows in all your expressions, in your behaviour, in your walk, in your talk, in your gestures, in your whole life. One thing you can never fully hide is love. You can hide anger to a great extent, you can eat anger inside you, you can put a big smile on your face. People may not notice your anger, your vengeance -

but you cannot hide love. It comes flooding from your eyes, your smile and your gestures. There are no rules on how to express love, because when you are in love, you cannot do a mistake. A lover is beyond all rules, beyond all scriptures, beyond all theories and philosophies.

Yet, Narada says in the next Sutra :

Bhavatu nishchaya dadhrya durdhvam shastra rakshanam

Yes, certainly a devotee is beyond all rules, because for a devotee the Divine is the only goal, the only concern. A devotee has nothing of his or her own. Yet you need to follow the scriptures in order to preserve and protect the scriptures and in order to honour the tradition. The tradition needs to be maintained and devotees have always followed. Although it doesn't mean anything to them, it doesn't matter to them, yet one honours the tradition, the injunctions; one honours certain rules.

Anyatha patitya ashankaya

Otherwise there is a possibility of falling out of it. If you don´t follow certain codes of conduct, there is a possibility that you will fall out of that love. *Anyatha patitya ashankaya* - there is the possibility to fall off the knowledge, off the path of love. So just follow and stick to these rules. This is very, very beautiful. No doubt you need freedom to blossom in love, but in turn love brings freedom in all situations, all circumstances. Nothing will be stifling, nothing will be bonding to you, nothing will restrict you, your freedom, in the true sense of love. Are you getting what I am saying?

When you are in love, nothing is a burden to you. When nothing is a burden, how can anything take away the freedom from you? You lose freedom when something is a burden to you. So love in turn brings that freedom. When a rule is imposed on you by someone else, then it is restricting to you. But when you have taken a rule on yourself, on your own, it is not any restriction, it is not suffocating to you. Like when you take on the rule of driving on the right side of the road, then that is it.

Discipline (rules) bring more freedom to us although, on the surface, it appears to restrict freedom. But if you go a little deeper, you will see that your own rules, your own disciplines bring you freedom. Though you are beyond all discipline, yet it is good to have your own discipline. Though it doesn't matter to you what you do, when you rise, what you eat etc., it is better to have a certain discipline because that gives you such freedom.

Lokopi tadeva bhojanadi vyapara stvasharira dharanavadhi

Our body is bound by discipline, it is bound by some clock. Whether you want it or not, whether you like it or not, your system gets tired at some time, wants to sleep at some time, a definite time, is hungry at a definite time, it goes for nature calls at a definite time. Your body is in certain discipline as long as we are in this body, on this planet, with people around us. We need to honour the rules, honour the discipline, honour whatever rules, in whichever place. Here, (Lake Tahoe, Montreal), driving on the right-hand side is the rule. If you go to India or England, it is left-side driving and you have to honour that rule there. Honouring the rules, the Shastras, the scriptures brings you enormous freedom and freedom sustains love; love in turn brings you enormous freedom, the true freedom. Nothing can take away the freedom that love brings you - not the mind. There is a subtle difference. Be in the world like anybody else, like a common, ordinary person. Be one with everyone in the world, in society.

Tallakshanani vachyante nana matbhedat

Different rishis, different traditions spoke about this Divine love and its characteristics. But they are all different - different perceptions.

The Truth is the same but they saw different characteristics.

Poojadishu anurag iti Parasharyah

Parashara, one of the pioneers of the Vedic tradition, said, "A deep interest in Pooja is a sign of Divine love." What does Pooja mean? It is not just a ritual. 'Poo' means fullness, 'Ja' means that which is born out of fullness. When you are so full and you are so grateful, what you do from that state of mind, of existence, is Pooja. And how is Pooja done? Not just using limited mind, but using the entire universe, all the five elements and the Soul, the Mind and the Being. And offering of the totality is Pooja. An intense interest in Pooja is one of the characteristics of devotion, of Bhakti. A sense that comes up in you that you want to offer every little bit of what you are or what you have. "I have been given this universe, now I offer the universe back. I have been given this body and every particle of this body, I am offering back to you. You gave me this world and I offer this back to you. And I am yours." This intense feeling of offering, merging, giving everything to the Divine - every bit of it is called Pooja. An intense interest or liking for Pooja is one of the signs, one of the characteristics of such a deep devotion - a total offering, not saving something for oneself, becoming the offering itself, is Pooja.

Kathadishviti Gargah

The Rishi Garga said Katha, meaning story - talking about the glory of it. Listening and talking about it. When you are in love with someone, you want to know everything about them. What do they do? Where do they sit? Where did they go? What do they think? What is their opinion? What do they say? You want to know everything about them. And an interest in listening to that story and telling the story of the beloved is another characteristic of such a deep devotion, such a deep love. No other subject interests you.

When you are in love, you only talk about the beloved and the beloved's stories. This is another sign, another characteristic of such Divine love. In nothing else is there any interest - *kathadishviti Gargah*.

Atmarati avirodhena iti Shandilyah

Another Rishi by the name Shandilya says a characteristic of love is rejoicing in the Self without any conflict. This is a sign of Divine love. The moment you are happy, immediately a conflict arises in you, "Oh I shouldn't be happy." Society has stuffed so much guilt in you. And you cannot be at peace having guilt in your heart. But when you are in love, such deep love with this existence, with all the people on this planet, there is no way you can have any guilt. Guilt is always associated with selfishness, with self-pleasure. Guilt cannot be with sacrifice and love is sacrifice. Wrong understanding imposes guilt in you. *Atmarati* means reposing in the Self, being in the Self, rejoicing in the Self without any conflict. To cross the conflict you need wisdom, you need grace. Shandilya's way to look at Divine love is reposing, rejoicing in the Self without any conflict. And love brings you that. Divine love, Supreme love makes you rejoice in the Self without any conflict.

Having enunciated what other Rishis say, now Narada comes to his own way of looking at Divine love. He says :

Naradastu tadarpitakhilacharita tadvismarne param vyakulteti

But my opinion is *tadarpitakhilacharita* - offering all my actions, all my attitudes, all my tendencies because it is the actions, tendencies and intentions which stop you from rejoicing in the Self. And all that hinders me to rejoice in the Self, I offer them all to the Divine. And when I forget the Divine, becoming extremely uncomfortable is the real characteristic of Divine love. Narada says forgetfulness of the Divine causes intense pain, intense longing, intense restlessness - this is the characteristic of Divine love.

Astyevamevam

It is like that.

Yatha vraj gopikanam

Like it happened to the Gopis of Brindavan. The Gopis had nothing of their own. Every move they made was for the Divine, their mind, their heart, their soul was all immersed in Lord Krishna. It is like that, like the Gopis of Brindavan. How they were utterly in dismay, when, even for a moment, they forgot their beloved. And how everything that they did was only with one thought, "How would my Lord appreciate this? What would he want? How would he like this?" This was in their mind all the time. Whether they sang, they cooked, they churned the butter or they danced and dressed, they did everything for one reason - how would my lord appreciate this? It is for the love. There are ample number of stories about Gopis and their love and devotion towards Krishna. Narada says that is a sign of Divine love. There is a story…

Once Lord Krishna had a headache and all the doctors came but they could not find the reason for his headache. No medicine would work. Krishna said one medicine would work, "If the dust from the feet of any one of my devotees is applied on my head, my headache will go." Were there no devotees in Dwarka, in the place where he was? Many people were there, but how many would put the dust of their feet on his head, because the scriptures say that if you put the dust of your feet on the Lord, then you will go to hell. It is a sin and nobody wanted to go to hell. Then Krishna sent one of his messagers, Udhava, to Brindavan. As soon as he came, all the Gopis asked him, "Oh, tell me, what is the news in Dwarka? How is Lord Krishna? Is everything okay?" "He is fine," the messenger replied, "but he has a headache." A cry arose, "He has a headache! Are there no good doctors there? Are there no Vaidyas there?" He told them that they are there but the medicine was not available. "What is that medicine?" they asked, "Come on tell us, what can we do?" He said that he needed the dust of the feet of devotees. "How much do you want? Take truck-loads!" Udhava reminded the Gopis that if they put the dust from their feet on the head of the Lord, they would go to hell. "Never mind, even if we have to go to hell, have to be in hell for thousands of years, fourteen thousand years - we don't mind. You take the dust. We can't bear our Lord having a headache!" There was not a bit of selfishness in the love of the Gopis. The 'I', 'I' had totally dissolved. They existed as though they were not - so hollow and empty. And there are many such stories - the love of the Gopis with Krishna is something unique. It is one depiction of what Divine Love is.

Tatrapi na mahatmya gyan vismrityapavadah

Often, love and respect are in conflict. Respect needs a certain distance and love cannot tolerate any distance. Often when people come together, when they have so much love, they lose respect for each other. And there is a conflict in trying to gain the respect. Finally, they have neither respect nor love - they loose both. Most marital problems end up like this, because there is a need for love and there is a need for respect, too. But they are seemingly opposite. It is only in Divine love that respect also grows and love also grows. The closer you come, the more respect you get and the farther you go, the more love you experience. Distance is not a factor in Divine love, in the love which is fully blossomed. Such was the love of the Gopis.

Tatrapi na mahatmya gyan vismrityapavadah - they did not forget the greatness, the respect, the glory which belongs to you. That which is part of you seems to lose its glory. But in Divine love the glory increases. You do not forget the glory, the closer you get.

That is a sign of enlightenment, of knowledge, of wisdom, of blossoming in love. Love cannot tolerate distance and respect cannot do away with distance. Divine love is a combination of love and respect and both are totally nurtured.

Tadviheenam jarannamiva

Without that love, without that respect, the love is worth nothing. It is like the love of prostitutes. A prostitute is not interested in giving pleasure to the person, is not happy when the other person is happy, but is only worried about her income; what she will get out of it. If love comes with a bargain, "What will I get out of it, what do I get being devoted to God, what I get by doing this..." then, it is like the love of a prostitute. Yes, he has used a very strong word.

Nastyeva tasmin tatsukh sukhitvam

The Gopis said that we are here for your pleasure, we have come here because you would like to see us - not because we want to see you. There was no demand of any sort there, there was no complaint. "All that we want is your comfort; what is it that you want? We are here for you." That is the love of the Gopis. "Our only intention is to make you comfortable and whatever it takes, we are ready. We are here for that."

Nastyeva tasmin tatsukh sukhitvam - rejoicing in this, in the comfort of the Beloved is the sign of Love. If you examine, if you keenly look into the experience of love that you all have had, you will find all these characteristics hiding here and there. It is all there, it only needs a little watering, a little enrichment. Love cannot be devoid of these characteristics. You do have them, you only need to nurture them a little. And that is why these Sutras - the threads.

For a kite to go high, it needs a little thread.
This knowledge, this wisdom is such thread.

Significance of Pooja

Om Namoh Bhagavate Vasudevaya
Om Namoh Bhagavate Vasudevaya
Om Namoh Bhagavate Vasudevaya

In Karnataka, in the south of India, in the months of October/November there is a festival 'Aida Pooja' when people worship everything - shoes, instruments, buses, cycles, cars, scooters and trucks - they feel grateful for all these inanimate objects. See, these are the things that make our lives comfortable, so they are grateful for them. They will put flowers on the buses, and they will prostrate in front of the bus.

They worship all the instruments, knives and stoves. I remember my grandmother - in the night she would clean the stove. The stove used to be an earthen stove in the village. She would clean the stove and the next morning she would make some designs on it and then worship the stove first, then ignite fire and worship the fire. And then keep a pot on it with water and worship the pot. You go to collect the water from the well, first you worship the well and then take the water from it - so practically everything becomes worshipful. You know as kids we used to make so much fun -"She is prostrating before the stove which she has not even ignited !"

If you cannot see God in everything in this universe, you are not going to see him anywhere else. That Divinity needs to be recognised. A guest is honoured and worshipped - buses and

31

trucks, cycles and scooters are all cleaned and decorated with flowers - sometimes they decorate the windshield with so many flowers, the driver cannot even see what is in front! But, trust in God you know (laughter) and drive! Here in America, we trust in God in the dollar bill, but there the trust in God is in peoples' mind. The divine is present everywhere. When the Divine is present everywhere, what is wrong in adoring anything?

People ask me, " Why do people worship you so much?" I say, "It is up to them. If they see God in me, which they cannot but see, it is their choice. I see in them, too." I say, "Wherever you begin, don't stop there - worship everybody, worship everything, honour everything." Today there is violence in the world because they have not taught people how to honour life. Honour each other, honour life, wherever it is - in the dog, in the donkey, in the cow. The ancient rishis were simply amazing. They connected animals with Divinity - Gods, Devas...Kala Bhairava, they connected Bhairava with a dog. They connected each Divinity with a tree, with an animal, to show you that God, human beings, animals, trees all belong to one family, one universal family.

Also, always worship yourself. Establish Divinity in each part of your body. Puja begins with adoring each part of the body, for this body also belongs to the Divine. In the Christian tradition, in the Catholic tradition, also, it is there - you make a sign of the cross and then say, "The father, the son and the holy ghost - let them all be in this body." Honour the body and honour the universe - that is Pooja. We need to bring these values back in society.

Society need to flourish in love - worship is inevitable, adoration is inevitable.

32

Om Namoh Bhagavate Vasudevaya
Om Namoh Bhagavate Vasudevaya
Om Namoh Bhagavate Vasudevaya

Love is multi-dimensional. It is vast and enormous. Love is magnanimous and so many sages have viewed it from many different angles. And they glorified one aspect of love. Worship is one such aspect - Pooja or worship. In a society which is bound with ego, worship is looked down upon. Worship is considered a sin in an ego-bound society. Honouring is considered to be something not very nice in a stiff and competitive society. But in a society or in an institution where love is honoured, love blossoms. Honouring, worshipping is held very high. In the East, you can find people honour the trees. They worship trees, they worship people. People worshipping people are looked down upon in the West. Honouring someone seems to take out someone's prestige or self-esteem. But in the East the value is completely different, the one who is honouring gains more prestige. What they honour doesn't matter. You may honour a cow, you may honour a snake, you may honour or worship a tree. But the value of the one who is honouring goes up. The worshiper is glorified, not what he worships, because the worshiper exhibits the quality of his own consciousness. If you praise someone, it is your generosity, your magnanimity that comes through in the praise. There is a proverb in Sanskrit which says,

"Gods praise each other, human beings simply live in peace and demons curse each other, they blame each other."

One of the characteristics of Love is worship, adoring. When people are in love with any celebrity, they adore them, they worship them. It just indicates the degree of love. One who is in love with this entire universe would worship everything in this universe. Because every little bit that is in this existence is part of one Divinity. And worshipping this universe only makes you more Divine. God worships you every day, the Divinity is worshipping you every day. That is what Pooja is. This existence is offering you flowers, it is offering you fruits, it is offering you grains, and it is taking the Sun and the Moon around you. It is doing *aarti* to you. (They call it *aarti* when you light camphor, or a wick or a candle and move it around the altar.) The Divine is doing your Pooja every day. The worshipper and the worshipped become one, that union is love. Adoring the Divinity in all the forms is Divine love.

It begins with you, where you are. Worship is condemned in a society which is individualistic and which is ego-centric. But in a society, which honours the entire existence, which honours every little thing in this world, worship is adored and held high. Adoration is one of the signs of love.

The second sign of love is talking about it constantly, praising it. A newborn baby in the house is such a joy for the grandparents and they won't stop talking about it. And the same is with the parents, "Oh, look at the baby, 2, 3 months old baby, wished Jai Guru Dev, she folded her hands. She looked and you know, she said this, she said that, she recognizes this, she recognizes that. I was wearing a new outfit and the baby looked at me and said it is so nice. (Laughter) These are all the imagination of parents and grandparents. And they all say they have seen so many kids, but nothing like this baby. For them the baby is beyond anything in this world. That adoration...you should see the spark in their eyes when talking about their kids. They don't mind if the other person is listening or not. They don't even see that the guests to whom they are talking are thoroughly bored. But they don't stop talking about their babies. Their baby is the best and the cutest, the most intelligent baby in the whole world. Never has something like that happened ever before. Parents feel like that, grandparents feel like that, isn't that so?

Kathadishviti Gargah - that is another sign of love. Talking about your story, your passion - that is what you keep talking about.

Atmarati avirodhena iti Shandilyah - the Rishi Shandilya is known for just breaking all the rules. (Laughter) When no other rule fits, then that is called *Shandilya Shastra*, that means its own rule. You can find such rules in the streets of Calcutta, in India - everyone can drive the way they want, left, right or centre; anyway you want, you can drive.

Rejoicing without conflict. The moment joy comes in life, suddenly you feel guilty, "Oh, I shouldn't be enjoying this, no, no, I shouldn't feel good about me. I shouldn't praise myself." And if someone praises you, you feel an expansion. As soon as you feel that expansion, suddenly something happens and you say, "No, no I shouldn't be feeling like that, this is ego." You think you are boosting your ego. These types of conflicts put you down. Self blame is the worst thing that can happen to a seeker on the spiritual path. If you blame yourself, how can you ever go near you? Because you never want to go to something which you blame, which you dislike. So if you blame someone, you cannot be one with them. And if you blame yourself, you cannot go deep into yourself. You cannot get in touch with yourself, your centre. In our society, we have made so many arrangements to feel bad about ourselves, blame ourselves - so much guilt, calling yourself a sinner and a hopeless person, good for nothing. And we think that this is humility. The so called humility we practice is nothing but boosting the ego in an indirect way. It is not humility at all. In the name of virtue, in the name of humility, we try to put conflict in our consciousness. In the name of service, in the name of love, unknowingly we are creating more conflict in our consciousness. Then you can never settle peacefully within yourself. Meditation cannot happen within you.

But once the Divine love has caught in you, the spark has come, then the conflict resolves and you settle so deep - this is another sign of Divine love. Okay, if this is not happening, conflicts are still existing, what do you do? Narada gives the best solution:

Naradastu tadarpitakhilacharita tadvismarne param vyakulteti - then offer everything, offer all your negative feelings. By offering negative feelings, you feel relieved. And, he says, offer all positive feelings, offer all virtues. Offering all virtues you are relieved of the burden of feeling somebody special, getting into an ego trip. There can be two egos, the negative part of the ego and the positive part of the ego - that identification. Ego simply means limited identity and love is unlimited expansion. That is why ego and love are always in conflict. Ego is limited boundary and love is an expansion which moves towards unlimitedness, unboundedness. So what to do? The limited things you offer to the unlimited, to the Divine. Dissolve the boundaries in the vastness of the space and offer them.

You can see boundaries when your head is down on the ground, but when you lift your head up, the sky has no boundaries. It is moving from mud to the consciousness, to the vastness of intelligence. Your body has boundaries, but your spirit has none. The spirit is like the sky, body belongs to this earth. The spirit belongs to the vast expansion, the big mind, the Divinity. So offer all your actions, your thoughts, your tendencies to the Divine. And our actions, our tendencies are a combination of matter and spirit. Spirit alone cannot act, matter alone cannot act. The combination of spirit and matter, which is life, brings forth all the activity, good or bad, pleasant or unpleasant. Offer them all to the Divine - *tadarpitakhilacharita.*

Forgetfulness of one's nature is misery. You are miserable when you are away from your nature, because your nature is love. You are love - *tadvismarne param vyakulteti*. That is again a sign of love. If you are extremely restless, if you are feeling uncomfortable in your life, it simply shows that you have forgotten the Divine love. Doing everything else is simply beating around the bush. If you are in anguish, it is simply because you do not remember the Divine love that is in you.

Well, all this sounds very nice, but it sounds a bit airy-fairy, not very practical in life. (Laughter) It is all very good, nice as a theory, but what to do in life? Is it possible? Is it practical? Narada says, yes, yes, yes.

Yatha vraj gopikanam - if the Gopis could have it, you, too, can have it. Gopis were very simple maids, they were not scholars, they were not intellectuals. Neither did they do a lot of penance or practices. They were very simple household women. And if they could have it, you can have it, too. It is possible, it is practical - such a love can dawn in you. Wake up, don't under-estimate yourself. Your love is unconditional, your love does not depend on your external situations, circumstances or people. Like you can breathe anywhere, wherever you are, can't you? You don't need a condition in order to breathe. You can blink your eyes anywhere. Like blinking your eyelids, like taking a deep breath - such simple actions of your existence. Love is even simpler than that, because that is what you are.

Love and business are opposite in their nature. In love, you give more and take just little bit, just for exchange. In business, you give a little bit and take more. They don't go together. Business is a subject of your head and love is a subject of your heart. They have completely opposite values. You should never do business with your heart and love from your head. When you are in love, don't go on

37

judging, don't be manipulative in love - you will destroy love. But when you are doing business, don't do it from your heart. You will be a failure in your business. Keep them in their place - you cannot mix soup and ice cream. You can have them in the same meal, but a little apart. You have to keep them apart otherwise you will neither be able to enjoy the ice cream nor the soup. Love and respect need to be enriched in life. The greatness and glory need to be appreciated. Each particle in this universe exhibits the glory of the Divinity. Look at the variety in this creation. If you keep looking at the variety, where is the time to worry? Where is the time to sit and grumble? So many types of people, so many types of flora and fauna, so many types of animals. You can be busy the whole time, appreciating, wondering about this universe!

In love, the gopis never forgot the glory. Often, when one is in love, one starts demanding, one starts feeling jealous about the other. Jealousy, demand, anger, all these come when you do not keep your beloved on a higher pedestal. When you put the Divine on a higher pedestal, then there is a sense of surrender, then there is a sense of submission and there is a sense of unconditional love. That is called *mahatmya*, the greatest, the glory. Often, when you glorify someone, you just idolize them, but there is no love connection between you and them. You only love those who are on your same level. You cannot love someone above you; you simply appreciate them, glorify them. But you cannot feel that oneness, the connection, because you feel that there is a distance. "Oh, they are up there, how can I be one with them? Then how can I be one with God? How can I be one with the prophet? How can I be one with the saint? He is a saint and I am just a normal human." When you put yourself down, you cannot have a total communication, a total rapport. That becomes a hindrance.

But when you feel one with them, then all this other paraphernalia of negativity begins. Demand comes and you forget the glory. In spite of having such a personal love for the Lord, for Krishna, in spite of having such oneness, friendliness, the Gopis never forgot the glory aspect. They did not forget the greatness. This is a combination of greatness and intimacy that you see in Buddha, in Krishna, in Jesus, in the Prophet. The closer you go, the glory never diminishes, it only increases. When you are centred, the closer a person comes to you, they appreciate you even more. When you are not centred, the closer they come, they start losing respect for you.

Love and business need to be kept apart. If they are mixed, it will be like prostitution. In that nobody gains any pleasure, nobody gains any happiness. Divine love on one side and prostitution on the other hand are the extremities of the band of love.

Sa tu karma gyana yogebhyah api adhiktara

This love is higher than action, higher than any service that you may do.

Service done without love is of no use. People do a lot of service - they work in Red Cross, in hospitals, do this and that; you may do many good things to people, good actions - but Divine love is higher than action.

Knowledge - you may be a wonderful yogi, you maybe doing the highest form of meditation, yoga, practices, but, he says, it is much higher than people who are engaged in action, people who are engaged in knowledge and people who are engaged in yoga - *karma gyana yogebhyah api adhiktara.*

That does not mean that one who is in Divine love is just in a mood - "I am in Divine love - no need for any yoga, any meditation, any service.." No, he says, thay are all aids to you.

Glorify the Divine

Phala roopatvat

Ishwarasya api abhimana dweshitvat dainyapriyatvat cha

Tasyah gyanameva sadhanamityeke

Anyonya ashrayatvam iti anye

Swayam phala roopateti brahmakumarah

Rajagriha bhojanadishu tathaiva drishtatvat

Na tena raja paritoshah kshuchchantirva

Tasmaat saiva grahya mumukshubhih

Tasyah sadhanani gayantyacharyah.

Tat tu vishayatyagat sangatyagat cha

Avyavrat bhajanat

Loke api bhagavad guna shravana keertanaat

Mukhyatastu mahatkripyaiva bhagavatkripa leshad va

Mahatsangastu durlabhagamyo amoghascha

Labhyate api tatkripyaiva

Tasmin tat jane bhedabhavat

Tadev sadhyata tadeva sadhyataam

Dusangah sarvathaiva tyaajyah

Om Namoh Bhagavate Vasudevaya
Om Namoh Bhagavate Vasudevaya
Om Namoh Bhagavate Vasudevaya

Surrender often denotes a sense of weakness, a sense of failure, a sense of slavery, isn't it so? But there is another part of surrender. That aspect of the word "surrender" which denotes freedom. The pinnacle of Love is also called "surrender" - where your whole Being becomes one with the infinite, where the river meets the ocean, where the activity reposes in rest, in the self. The culmination of activity, the culmination of feeling, the culmination of action, of a moment, of an event is all called "surrender".

Surrender simply means from limited power energy to unlimited ocean of existence. Growing from limitation to limitless, merging into the divinity, the vast powerful omnipresent, omnipotent truth. An intense love is associated with surrender. Normally the word surrender is used with intense fear, anguish, weakness. Actually a weak person cannot surrender. He will appear to have surrendered, but inside there is a deep-seated desire to take revenge, to come back with more vengeance. Only when you realize your magnanimity can you be at peace. That state you call surrender, that merging with the Divine. Often surrender has been used as something to convey slavery or weakness. When you let go of all the tension, fear, anxiety and small mindedness, what dawns in you is freedom - that freedom is real joy, is real love, is the

40

beauty, and that could be called surrender. It is in your nature. It is in heaven and it is in your nature. Like the mother's love for her baby, 6 months, 1 year, 2 year old baby - you can say the mother surrenders to her baby.

Narada's entire aphorisms focus on offering all activities, all attitudes, everything to the Divine and feeling free. If you are miserable, then you have forgotten your true nature. No one else is responsible for your misery because it is just you who has forgotten how vast, how beautiful you are. You know a small speck of dust can obstruct your vision of vastness, can't it? You are looking at the vast sky, a huge mountain - just a small dust particle in your eyes is enough to blind you. In the same way, completely insignificant things occupy your mind. Really useless things occupy your mind, go round and round, and obstruct your true nature, which is love.

Is love a practice? No. Can you sit and practice being in Love? How many days, how many minutes? How should you sit and what should you do? Raise your arm up and tongue out? There was a gentleman in one of the meditation classes. He was the chief justice in the international court at Hague. After hearing all the talk on how meditation means to be effortless - nothing to do, just to relax, at the end of it, he asked where the tongue should be! "What should be the position of the tongue when we meditate?" I said as long as it is inside the mouth, it is okay! (Laughter) Where do you put the tongue? Keep it out?

Effortlessness. Virtues are there in you, do not try to cultivate virtues - they are in you already. All that you need is to become a little quiet, a little calm. When you become effortless, calm and serene, virtues, talents and skills all manifest in your life, all come to the surface. All our effort is only to get rid of the stress, get rid of all the dust that we have accumulated. And *Karma* - our action, *Gyana* - knowledge,

41

and *Yoga* are all a way, a path to do this, to achieve this purity. Actually, 'achieve' is not the correct word. Knowledge is like a detergent - to be put on and then washed off! Same way with action, "I did so much good," "I did this charity," "I did that charity." If you keep thinking this way, taking pride in your charity or the good work you have done, then that becomes a deterrent to your blossoming. There is a proverb in Hindi that says, "Do good and throw all the merit in the well, throw it in the river."Don't even remember what good things you have done in life.

Have you heard the story about the emperor in China? Once Bodhisattva was invited to China, so he went from India. The Emperor of China welcomed him at the border. He gave him a big reception. In the reception, the minister of the emperor read out all the good that the king had done, all the charity work, dug many ponds and wells, made so many homes, donated so much money, and this and that, everything. And Bodhisattva, hearing everything, then told the Emperor, "You are going to go to hell." At his very first step into the land of China, at the very first reception, he says, "You are going to go to hell because you are taking pride in the good works you have done. You are taking pride in charity." "Oh, I have served so many people." This is like holding on to the detergent. You know, if you don't wash away the detergent, the soap that you leave on your clothes, that itself will become dirt, whether it is knowledge or the good work or actions that you do. Nor can you say, "I meditated over 20 years." For whose sake did you meditate 20 years? You seem to take a sense of pride in having meditated 20 years. You complain, "20 years I meditated, nothing is happening." Who is responsible? "I did this, this, this and nothing happened to me." Your spiritual practices should not make you complain about some result that you may want to achieve. Narada says that Divine Love is a greater high than all. Why? Because it is the fruit. If you are doing some good job, the fruit of it is imminent, it is immediate. It gives you a sense of fulfilment, right then and there.

Love is not a means to some ends. Do not ever make love a

42

means. It is an end in itself and the same is with faith. You know, the amount of comfort faith gives you, nothing else can give you. If you have faith, the faith itself is the end. Often, we also use faith as a means, love as a means. Be grateful that you have faith. Don't try to cash in on faith. "Oh God, I have so much faith in you, what are you doing to me?" God will say, " Well, if you have faith in me, it is up to you. What do I get from your having faith in me? More headache! Whenever you call, I have to be there."You try to cash in on every little good attitude that you have in life. Because we make all this as a means to some end.

Faith itself is an end. Love itself is the fruit - it is the end.

One moment of such a love, such ecstacy in life, that taste of complete love, pinnacle of Love, is worth our entire life. That is good enough. If a few drops of tears have fallen from your eyes in love, that is worth your life. This is an end in itself. Love is the end in itself. Faith is the end in itself - not a means. But our mind is so clever, it wants everything to have some illusion of comfort or pleasure. No doubt faith brings comfort, but if you are intelligent, you will not try to use it for comfort. It is like selling diamonds to buy a bottle of Coca Cola. (Laughter) Offering finger chips...selling a bag full of diamonds to buy a packet of french fries!

Phala roopatvat - that Divine love is itself an end, is itself the fruit.

Ishwarasya api abhimana dweshitvat dainyapriyatvat cha - Even to God pride is not palatable.

See, God loves these two instances. When a doctor tells a patient, "Don't worry, I'm here. I will take care of you"or when someone says, "I own this piece of property" - God has a big laugh. *Ishwarasya api abhimana dweshitvat dainyapriyatvat cha* - the ego simply indicates a lack of awareness, a narrow understanding. If there is no

43

understanding at all , then, also, there is no ego problem. And if there is full understanding, there is also no ego. Ego comes up when there is a partial understanding, half Knowledge. Humility is what nature loves. Ego is stiffness, humility is being like a feather. Humility is lightness, ego always makes you very heavy. Why do you have to prove to yourself that you are correct all the time? Just let life be. Just knowing. That is how it is. Accept it. Being with the current, flowing with the current - that is wisdom, that is *Gyana.*

Tasyah gyanameva sadhanamityeke

But how to be humble, how to have that humility? Only through Knowledge - this is what some people say. In this vast universe, what are you? Who are you? You are nothing, you are nobody. So many billions like us have come. They have walked this planet and they have all gone. And there are billions waiting in the queue. They are all going to come. You are just on the conveyor belt, passing by. You are nobody. Just look at your life from the vast expanse of time and space. You will come into a big realization that you are nobody. And that brings the quality of humility in your consciousness.

When humility is lacking, all communications break down. You cannot communicate with someone who is not humble. Humility keeps the communication open with everyone. With humility you can link with people of all levels, of all creeds, of all age groups, of all standards, of all class of people. When you treat everyone like dust and you think that you are somebody, that you are so intelligent, you are so much more brilliant than everybody, then I tell you, nature laughs at you "You poor thing, how foolish you are." Don't see everyone else as dust, see yourself as dust.

You know, when I was in school, there were so many intelligent boys and girls in my class. And all of them thought, "I am going to be somebody." Do you know, the dull students have done much better

44

than them. They are doing very well in their lives, better than all the intelligent students.

Nature has its own plans. In every heart, the Lord resides. Honour everyone, respect everyone - humility will bring that in you. Your good deeds, your Knowledge, skills, can all give you such pride, that you are *somebody*. The best Knowledge can bring you an awareness that you are *nobody*. So many people say that only through Knowledge can you cultivate humility - no, not cultivate, only through knowledge can you *enliven* that humility. But some other people say that they depend on each other - love and humility.

Love and Knowledge go hand in hand.

Anyonya ashrayatvam iti anye

Others say it depends on each other. Knowledge and love, they go together. Only when you have love, do you take interest in Knowledge, you like to know about it. Suppose you have no love for astronomy, would you ever become an astronomer? Can you be a good astronomer? Not possible. If you love physics, then you can be a good physicist. So because of love, you gain knowledge; because there is knowledge, then you grow more in it. So they complement each other. But, again I tell you -

Swayam phala rupateti Brahmakumarah

Love is the final. Love is the fruit. Love is the end.

Any amount of Knowledge you may have got, all the Knowledge leads you to love. You may go to a swimming pool, you may go onto a diving board, but you have to let go of the diving board, you have to jump into the water. Whether you jump on this side or that side, any corner, but you have to jump. If you go to a swimming pool and you hold onto the board, can you swim? If you hold onto the railing, can

45

you jump into the water? No!

Rajagriha bhojanadishu tathaiva drishtatvat
Na tena Raja Paritoshah kshudh Shantirva

Just by reading the menu card, your hunger cannot be satisfied, can it? Similarly, just by looking at the architectural plan of a home, can you relax in your home? Just with the plans there? Same way, simply having Knowledge is not sufficient. Love is needed, the experience is needed. Simply reading is not sufficient, but the experience alone will quench. Knowledge is like reading the menu card, love is experiencing it.

Tasmat saiva grahya mumukshubhih

And so, those who are desirous of liberation or freedom should only go for Divine Love. What does that mean? Have Knowledge, but immerse in Love. Just sing, dance, be drawn in ecstasy. Now how to do that? "Okay, I am ready to walk on the path of love. But what is it? How to do it?"

Tasyah sadhanani gayantyacharyah

The great teachers have sung the means for this. That is why these are called Sutras, *hints*, to you. They never give you advice that cannot be fruitful, which cannot be looked into, which cannot be attended to. The Rishis have never left you hanging in space; they have always understood where you come from, where you are, and how to guide you in the next step. Just like the mother takes care of the baby, the Master has always been taking care of seekers - what you get, what you cannot get; and how to get what you want, step-by-step, with patience and perseverance.

Tasyah sadhanani gayantyacharyah - *Acharyah* means one who gives a certain amount to everybody, one who cares for everyone.

Om Namoh Bhagavate Vasudevaya
Om Namoh Bhagavate Vasudevaya
Om Namoh Bhagavate Vasudevaya

Body and mind work on completely opposite laws. To build the body, you need to put effort. Effort is the language of the body whereas effortlessness, letting go, relaxing is the law with the mind. If you want to remember something, the harder you try, the longer it will take. But when you relax, you will remember easily. The mind needs no effort to develop. But that does not mean being lazy and just sleeping. If you want to learn how to play the guitar or sitar or to learn karate, you need to put effort. But if you want to appreciate something, if you are in love with something, if you like something, it does not need any effort. If you make an effort to love somebody, or like something, that effort itself will prove to be counter-productive. So there is nothing that you *must* love, you *must* like. It is impossible. No "must" or "should" applies when it comes to your feelings. "You must feel this way" is an erroneous concept.

So, the Rishis said, *tasyah sadhanani gayantyacharyah* - how to blossom in love; they sang the means, the methods. The methods are so effortless, like singing. True singing comes out effortlessly. To make an effort to sing is not as good; it doesn't carry that energy, that

47

power, that force. Singing must be effortless. That is why if you sing from your heart, you will never feel tired. But when you are exerting to impress someone else, then that effort you put in the singing brings exhaustion to you. *Satsang* is singing from your heart, from your feeling, which brings more energy into your system. Isn't that your experience? When you sing in Satsang, how do you feel afterwards? Your feel more energized, revitalized, lively. The Sadhanas (the practices) to uplift the Divine love in you, are all effortless, like music, like singing. Deep rest brings out all the virtues in you. Deep rest kindles the subtle feelings in you. See, when you are tired and agitated, that is when you are away from love, isn't that so? If you are not loving, it is because you are restless, agitated, you are tired, you are frustrated. In all this you are depleted, energy is drained. So, go to the source of energy, not through activity, but through deep rest. The next sutra says :

Tat tu vishayatyagat sangatyagat cha

From the time we wake up in the morning until we go to bed, all our senses are continuously engaged in the objects of the senses. Either you are seeing something, listening to something (music or something), or you are smelling, or eating. Or you are touching or feeling something. Constantly, you are engaged in the objects of the senses. Engaging in the objects of the senses drains the energy, it is spending the energy. If man were given 24 hours without sleep, he would use all the 24 hours in just engaging in the object of the senses. But nature has fortunately or unfortunately created something called sleep, wherein you shut all the senses out and drop deep into yourself. Without that you cannot exist, because you recuperate in sleep. When you withdraw your mind, your consciousness, from engaging in the objects of the senses, then you gain deep rest.

Once Mullah Naseruddin was galloping on his horse. He looked exhausted, tired. He couldn't even sit. He was lying flat on the back of the horse, hanging on to the horse. His face looked so dull and tired, his eyeballs rolling up. The horse was moving around and around the same streets in the village. People asked, "Hey, Mullah, where are you going?" He said, "I haven't the least idea. Please ask the horse." Our senses take us on such a gallop - we have no idea where we are going, what we are doing, what we want. I had a friend in school. He would turn the radio on and he would not listen to any station for even one minute. He would keep tuning, keep searching, moving from one station to another station, not even two sentences of a song would he listen to - he was so restless, he just could not keep from fiddling.

Similarly, we eat and we go on eating and eating. When you are asked what you ate, you don't even know what you ate. You sit on the couch watching television and you keep stuffing yourself. Suddenly you find there is nothing left in front of you. You've stuffed everything and what you ate, you have no idea, how much you ate, you have no idea. When people become restless, they keep on eating. They are not enjoying the food - it is just the feverishness to stuff things inside. It is a Catch 22 situation. When you are exhausted, you keep eating. And when you have eaten so much, you get exhausted, you can't do anything else.

Similarly, people go for sightseeing. You go to Paris, you go here and there, eyes wide open, looking at all the buildings. You come back tired and tanned, totally exhausted. What did you do? 'Sightseeing!' What did you see? 'Well, nothing.' Look at all the faces of tourists moving around, seeing this building, that building. Do they feel revitalized, energized, enthusiastic, bubbling with bliss and joy? No. Most of the holidays people take are tiring and exhausting - mentally, physically, emotionally, in all senses. After being on a holiday, they want to take another holiday. Coming back from a holiday, they want to rest a few days.

There cannot be rest unless you withdraw the senses from the objects. Deep rest is when you consciously withdraw all the senses

49

and take a conscious rest. Unconscious rest is inevitable, you have to sleep every night. Nature has designed our systems such that we need to do that, otherwise we would drop dead. But consciously bringing the mind away from the sense into its source, even for a few moments, brings such a deep rest in you. That is what is called *Vishayatyagat sangatyagat cha* - getting away from the objects of the senses. Bringing the mind back to its source will kindle the love that you are, will manifest the love that you are. You know, our senses have a limited capacity to enjoy. But the desire in the mind is unlimited. That is the cause for *bulimia*. You can only eat so much, but the mind is not satisfied. Your mind wants to just stuff things, more and more. How much can you stuff? Then you vomit. Then again you eat, then you throw up, then again you eat. Then you destroy this beautiful instrument, this body, by over using it, by misusing it.

Vishayatyagat sangatyagat cha - it is one thing to enjoy the object of the senses. Okay, you can listen to music, you can eat food, you can smell fragrance, you can enjoy touch and taste. But if it is in the mind, if you keep thinking all the time about the objects of the senses, then it is even worse. From morning till evening you just think about what food you are going to eat - this obsession cannot bring you rest. Obsession with sex, food, clothes or music, television or sightseeing, or anything, will only drain you of your precious energy. Are you getting what I am saying? Thinking about it constantly - obsession is not letting go; *vishayatyagat sangatyagat cha* - it is coming back to the source. This is one method. See, the objects of senses create an attraction in you, and if you immediately gallop on your attractions, that attraction does not bring fulfillment; it dies out and leaves you in a state of inertia. Any one sense, if you use it too much, will only cause inertia, dullness. If you are listening to music from morning to night, your brain will become one sided - only your left brain will function, the right brain will not function. You cannot think, logic dies out. You cannot perceive things properly. Your observation, your expression, everything suffers. And it is the same way with all other senses. If you are using any one sense too much, that particular sense becomes dull and ineffective. Moderation is required. And moderation can come when you retire back to the self. *Vishayatyagat sangatyagat cha* - get back to the source that you are. Next method is :

Avyavrat bhajanat

Uninterrupted sharing. The word *bhajan* means sharing. Sharing what? Sharing that which the Divine is. The Divine is peace and you are peace - you share that peace with the Divine. What is it that we can all share together? That is one sound. See, when we sing the same song or same sound, it resonates in the mind, but when we are thinking, each one will think differently. That is why singing is called Bhajan, because you can very easily share that with everybody. That same sound, *Om Namo Bhagavate Vasudevaya* everyone is singing. That is in every mind, in every consciousness. So if everyone is laughing, that is also Bhajan. Don't think that just singing is Bhajan. Everyone together just laugh, laugh your head off - really laughing, rolling on the floor. That is Bhajan, too.

Avyavrat bhajanat - constantly share all that you have, not that one day you do bhajans, one day you share, other days you don't. Have a sense of one-ness with everything - share yourself with the trees, the mountains, the sky, with people, with animals.

Sharing your life is bhajan.

Avyavrat bhajanat - uninterrupted sharing of all that you are.

Lokepi Bhagavadguna shravana keertanat

Also, in the world, praise the Divine. Sing the glory of the Divine in your day to day activity. *Lokepi* - in your daily activity, in your normal life, in your social life; *Bhagavadguna* - talking abut the

51

qualities of the Divine, the glory of the Divine; *shravana* - listening about it, hearing about it.

Often, the mind takes interest in scandals. Somebody said something is wrong, somebody is not okay - "Oh, tell me what it is, tell me more about it. What about that person? What happened to them? What did they say? How bad is the situation...?" Good news is no news, bad news is the news. Where there is some fight or problem, you take more interest there. People seem to take more interest when something is going bad rather than when something is good. That is how scandals gain more importance than creative work. The interest of people is in negativity. Just see, if someone tells you something nice, how do you listen to it? "Oh, is that so?" You brush it off. But if someone tells you some problem, you take a deep interest - "Tell me more." Then what happens? Just observe. Observe in any conversation, when someone comes to you with some negativity, they make that negativity more concrete. The sign of bad company is when you go to a person with some problem and you come back feeling the problem is greater than you thought. The sign of good company is when you go to a person with a problem and you come back feeling that it is light, it is not as bad as you thought. People either blame the world around them or blame the people and see everything as horrible, everything as bad, everyone as a cheat. You don't find anything good in the world, in society. It is not the sign of a devotee, of a lover.

Bhagavad guna shravana keertanat - do you want to get to your goal? Praise the Divine. Praise the Lord. And listen only to that. Grandmothers used to plug their ears if they heard anything bad about someone, "Shiva, Shiva, Shivaye - don't tell me anything bad about someone. Let these ears hear only good things. Let my eyes only see good things. Let my tongue speak only something which is benevolent to people, which will bring harmony, rather than break up people, society. Our human body is made to bring heaven on this earth. The human

52

body is meant to bring sweetness into this world, not spill venom. *Bhagavadguna shravana keertanat* - uplift the Divine quality in other people. It is easy to put down anybody, but it takes some guts, some intelligence, courage to uplift people, to bring out the Divine quality in those around you. By bringing out Divine qualities in others, you will see the Divinity deep inside you. You will be able to recognize it inside you. And praising anyone is praising the Divine. All praise any way goes to the Divine. All worship goes to only one because the creator is only one. Unfortunately, this has been mistaken thoroughly. More than half of the world is under the idea that if you praise or worship something, you are not doing that to God. If you worship the tree, it is not adoring God. Who created the tree? It is God who created the tree. So when you praise the tree, is it not adoring God? A painter has painted something - if you appreciate the painting, whom are you praising? The one who painted, isn't that so? Appreciating this world means appreciating the Lord of this world. Appreciating beauty anywhere is appreciating the beauty in the spirit.

All praise, all adoration goes only to one. In the world also, sing the glory; in the world, recognize the beauty. Glorify the Divine!

Every flower has to remind you of its origin.

Every human being reminds you of your own origin.

Every bird singing reminds you of that beauty of the Infinity.

See this Divinity and sing its glory in your day to day activity. There is another means :

Mukhyatastu mahatkrupyaiva bhagavatkrupa leshad va

Predominant of all this is the Grace of the Master, of Guru. Like a lit candle can light another candle, only one who has, can give. One who is free can free you, one who is love can kindle the love. Most important is the Grace of the Guru and even that you can only get when you have some Divine Grace. *Krupaleshad va* - with just a little bit, a tiny drop of Grace from God, you gain the merit of the

53

Grace of the Master, the Guru.

Mahatsangastu durlabhagamyo amoghascha

And such a company is difficult to get. Millions of people are there on this planet. Not everybody will get in touch with the one who has attained it. It is very difficult. And the Master, *Sadguru* does not come in all ages. He comes once in a while. *Durlabha* - it is difficult to get; *Agamya* - unfathomable is his being; *Amogha* - you cannot measure the depth or understand it easily.

You cannot understand the Master easily - it is very difficult to understand his depth, his ways. You may walk by a Jesus, a Buddha or a Krishna and you may not notice him at all. Where can you know him in your time? Many think Krishna was what he was, only a few knew him. Others thought he was just a king, mischievous and cute, too tricky, sometimes very unreliable. Krishna was considered very unreliable. And he would just smile and everyone would forget all their problems. But later, when they would go away from him, they would remember, "I went to scold him - I forgot!" People used to go to shout at him, but when they were in front of him, they returned with a smile. He would make everyone forget. That is why he was called *Manmohana*. The mind would just drop, everything would be forgotten. People who never recognized Jesus, asked him, "Are you really the son of God?" as though others are not the son of God. Everybody is the son of God, who is not? That is why Jesus said, "To our Father in Heaven." He did not say only *my father*, not your father. "All is prayer to our Father" means what? You are also the son of God. But I know I am son of God, you do not know. Better you know. That is what his message was, but not everybody could recognize him, understand him. They put him in the category of thieves, dacoits.

Durlabha - very difficult to find, to get. *Agamya* - unfathomable. *Amogha* - you cannot measure the depth or understand easily. You

54

cannot understand the Master easily - it is very difficult to understand his depth, his ways. You cannot say something that is similar, parallel to that Being. You cannot compare a Guru, an Enlightened one, with anyone else. There will be nobody you can see coming near that Being. *Amogha* - never think you can understand them.Impossible!

Labhyate api tatkripyaiva

And you cannot take credit that for doing this, this, this, you could get the company of the Divine, the Guru, or an Enlightened One. Even that is bestowed on you unconditionally. It has not come to you on your merits. You have done nothing to deserve it. Don´t think you deserve it. "Oh, I did this, this, this, I deserve this." You don't. It is not coming to you because you deserve it. It is coming because of their Grace, because of their love for you.

Tasmin tat jane bhedabhavat

Between him and his people there is no difference - like a mother defends a child, like a father defends his son or daughter. If someone fights with a young child, what do the parents say? "Why do you blame them?" They take it on themselves. If your Beloved is blamed, you take the blame on yourself. If your Beloved is praised, you enjoy that praise. You think that you are being praised. In the same way, adoring the Divine is the same as adoring his people. *Tasmin tat jane* - there is no difference, no division between the Divine and his people, between him and those who are totally his, 100% his.

Tadev sadhyatam tadeva sadhyatam

Strive for that, and strive for that alone. Put your attention on that, put your attention on that company, on that Grace. That alone will bring you all that you need, whether material or ethereal or spiritual. *Tadev sadhyatam tadeva sadhyatam* - it is not easy to understand a Guru. But every move of your Guru is to make you strong and uplift you. There are many stories, events and instances about Guru - we will talk about another time.

Om Namoh Bhagavate Vasudevaya
Om Namoh Bhagavate Vasudevaya
Om Namoh Bhagavate Vasudevaya

Dusangah sarvathaiva tyajyah

Shun bad company. What is bad company? That company which fuels negativity is bad company. Suppose you go and sit with a friend and pour out all your negativity and you come back feeling even worse. That is bad company. One who makes you believe in your negativity more strongly is bad company. You know, you go and sit with some friends, talk to them, discuss your problems and when you go away from them you feel lighter, feeling all your negativity is just an illusion. That is being in good company.

It is easy to get into bad company. There are people who fuel negativity. You say this is hopeless, they say, "Yes, yes, it is not hopeless, it is horrible." That is bad company, yes? In good company when you discuss your problems you move away from them feeling lighter, feeling that the problem is really not that big - it is nothing, it can be solved.

Dusangah sarvathaiva tyajyah - by all means, shun bad company. Because it is the company that you keep that builds you up. *Dusangah sarvathaiva tyajyah* - what does bad company do? It creates feverishness and obsession in you, brings in you more and more desires, more lust, anger and delusion. Then finally you find yourself in a big soup - so far from love. It is like concrete negativity,

56

frustration personified - and that is bad company.

Dusangah sarvathaiva tyajyah - in the beginning it will be nothing of course, but it sucks you in and when you get sucked into that type of company, it becomes like a hailstorm. You are unaware; without your knowledge you just sit in the darkness of negative company and start saying, "Oh, he's bad, he's no good." The other day someone said, "So-and-so is so jealous of me." Come on! Even if they are jealous of you, you don't recognize it! You know, recognizing someone's jealousy puts you down. If they are jealous, it is up to them. Thinking they are jealous of you makes you all worked up, doesn't it? "Everybody is picking on me!" Such an illusion!

Don't think anyone is bad. We say, "Oh that person is bad, this person is bad, shun this company!" No! The bad company is within you, it is not in the other person. Bad company refers to your attitude. In our Bangalore Ashram we have two teachers - anybody comes to one of these teachers with any complaint, he will blow it up. He will say, "I agree with you. Yes, you are right!" But the other teacher, whatever complaints come to him, he will make sure that people feel lighter about it.

Don't feel obliged to say yes to someone's negativity. This is another problem. When a friend comes and complains to you about anything, even the weather, you feel obliged to say 'yes' to that complaint and flow with them, rather than contradicting them. Isn't that so? How many of you feel that way? There is no rule to feel obliged to flow with their negativity. Obligation itself is an illusion. We shouldn't feel obliged to say anything. See, if you feel one with everybody, if you have so much love, you don't feel obliged at all. Obligation comes when you feel a little distance, right? If someone is really part of you, do you feel obliged? Absolutely not. I don't feel obliged to anybody for anything. Everyone is part of me, why should

I feel obliged for anything? Obligation is an illusion, it makes you feel loaded. You have a load on your head and that makes you behave unnaturally- it takes you away from reality. What do you say? When you feel obliged, then you feel obliged to say 'yes' to their negativity. Then you become bad company for someone.

Smile and be innocent. Smile from the core of your heart, then you will see all the negativity will fly off, like when the sun shines, the dewdrops vanish, the darkness vanishes. Your smile is the light in your life.

Stop fueling negativity, stop feeling obliged - then you are good company. Not only that, then you will be a good company to anybody. It needs skill to shun someone. When someone is so negative, if you just shun them, and say, "This is not right, what you are saying is hopeless," they will just shut up and they won't really feel lighter. You need skill to deal with someone's negativity. Are you getting what I'm saying? They will just stop communicating with you because they are so convinced about their negativity. Unless you say yes to them, they don't feel sympathetic. So you need skill to put down their negativity. That is Satsang. And when you come from this position you will see that whatever complaints they have, as soon as they are aware of that feeling, they start dissolving, they start feeling lighter.

Dusangah sarvathaiva tyajyah - it is the company which will pull you forward in life. Everyone needs good company to progress, isn't it so? The husband gets into a bad company or the wife gets into bad company - the seeds will rip the family. Of course, when people are living together four, five, six, seven years, some misunderstandings creep up in any relationship, somebody says something and there will be an argument.

Skill is needed to acknowledge the negativity, yet not agree with it. Acknowledge it, not agree with it, and then break it - like with a knife, remove it. And move on, feeling lighter. Your life on this planet is meant to bring peace and lightness to everyone's life, not to create more complications. What do you say? So, when you feel one with everybody, when you have that love for everyone, then you don't feel obliged. But you have to do it with skill.

Question : What is someone's complaints are legitimate?

Sri Sri : That is how everyone feels. When they complain, they feel their complaints are completely legitimate. Wake up and see. If you see through knowledge, you always get what you deserve. Nature has that principle, that truth.

Crossing the
Ocean of Maya

Dusangah sarvathaiv tyaajyah

*Kaama krodha moha smriti bhransha
budhinaasha sarvanaasha kaarantvat*

Tarangaita apime sangaat samudrayanti

Kustarati, kustarati, mayaam ?

*Yo sangah tyajati, yo mahanubhavam sevate, nirmamo
bhavati*

*Yo viviktasthanam sevate, yo lokabandha munmoolyati,
nistraygunyo bhavati, yogakshemam tyajati*

*Yat karmaphalam tyajati, karmaani sannyasyati, tato
nirdvando bhavati*

*Yo vedanapi sannyasyati, kevalam avichinna anuraagam
labhate*

Sa tarati sa tarati, sa lokaam sa taaryati

Om Namoh Bhagavate Vasudevaya
Om Namoh Bhagavate Vasudevaya
Om Namoh Bhagavate Vasudevaya

Dusangah sarvathaiv tyaajyah - shun bad company. There is a saying by someone, "If you want to know a person, know him through the company he keeps or the books he reads." Shun bad company. What is bad company? The company which solidifies your negativity is bad company.

You have some problem, you have a complaint, you go and you talk to someone and they make your beliefs more strong in that negativity - that is bad company. And you go to someone else with the same problem, same thought, same negativity, and they will just make you feel lighter and when you walk away from them you feel that the problem is not as big as you thought it was before. That is the right company.

Don't think people who agree with your grievances, with your problems, are your friends. They are not. Those people who make your negative feelings and your frustrations grow more and more in you may appear to be friends, but they are your enemies. They are bad company. Right company, good company, is that which makes you feel the problem is nothing. "It is solvable, it is simple, don't worry." They pump enthusiasm in you. Haven't you had this experience? Many people you talk to confirm your negativity while there are others who simply dissipate your negativity. Shun bad company if you want to grow in love, because bad company provokes ambition in you.

Kama krodha moha smriti bhramsha buddhi nasha sarvanasha karan tvat

Why should we get rid of bad company? Why should we not keep bad company? It says it brings lust or ambition in you, feverishness in you. "That person has a Rolls Royce; I, too, should have one. That person has this; I, too, should have that." And then behind ambition comes anger.

Actually, if you look into it, it is your own mind which is either your friend or your enemy. The negative tendency in your mind is your own enemy. Don't think it is in the other person. You can turn around the other person's mind too. If the other's mind is negative, you can break the ice there - you need the skill to do that.

Kama krodha moha smriti bhramsha budhi nasha sarvanasha karan tvat - bad company brings ambition, desire, frustration, anger and delusion. You build a whole castle in your mind about negativity - how things are, how people are, how the whole world is. Haven't you had this experience before in your life? You thought such and such a person is hopeless and you made a whole concept about him in your mind just by listening to someone else and then suddenly you found out that all your opinions and ideas about the person were false. They fell apart. Your opinions prove to be wrong. How many times in your life have your own opinions failed you? Yet we do not learn from our own past.

That company which gets you lost, which doesn't let you learn from your own experience, is bad company. You can gallop on such a horse forever without being aware of anything in your life. That is how people commit the same mistake over and over again and get totally dejected and depressed their whole life - and they do not even know that they are miserable. They are no doubt miserable and they make everyone around them miserable, isn't that so? That is bad company.

Kama krodha moha smriti bhramsha - they forget all about themselves. There is no memory of them left, of who they are, what they are, what they want, where they are heading. They have no idea who they were, how they were. All adults forget that they were teenagers once, and that they, too, had problems as teenagers. When they have teenage children, they think the children are not doing well. Every adult feels that the children don't listen - they forget that they, also, did not listen to their parents at a particular time.

Smriti bhramsha - when the delusion comes, the memory loss happens. You lose your memory, you lose the knowledge of who you are. *Buddhi nasha* - the intellect becomes clouded. When the intellect is hazy, not clear, not sharp, everything appears wrong. It is the intellect, the *buddhi*, that says, "This is good, this is not good; this is right, this is not right." That which is, that which brings short-term joy and long-term misery is bad. That which brings long-term joy and short-term misery is good. This is the definition of good and bad. Good brings long-term joy and short-term challenges, problems, and bad is something that brings long-term problems and short-term joy. It is the intellect which decides whether this is good or not good, and when the intellect, itself, is gone, everything is lost. When the discrimination power in you is lost, then you are totally lost.

This is what you will find if you go and talk to prisoners in jail. At the spur of the moment they lost their intellect and they lost everything. All crimes can only happen when the intellect or the discrimination is lost, and most of them lose it through bad company. That is why mobs create more violence. The individual person cannot do so much harm - in a mob they throw stones, put fire to buses and trucks and break things. The mob becomes more violent than a single individual person. It is the mob psychology - a mob is more violent because they lose their intellect, they lose their discrimination. That is why bad company is to be shunned. Good company is that which cheers you up, which elevates you, which brings a pleasant attitude and feeling within you. *Kama krodha moha smriti bhramsha buddhi nasha sarvanasha karan tvat .*

Tarangaita apime sangat samudrayanti

In the beginning it may be just like a small wave, a ripple, but when you are associating yourself with bad company continuously, it will become like an ocean. Don't think, "Oh, it is just one party there, just one little thing that I'm doing." No, that one little thing can just rip you. That is how alcoholics who have recovered from being an alcoholic get sucked back into it. It is just one party, one peg - these sort of justification they give; they go for one little party once in a while and then that's it, finished. And they end up again entering the rehabilitation centre.

Tarangaita apime sangat samudrayanti - it may begin as a small ripple but if you keep associating with it, it will become like an ocean. It will cloud your whole mind, your intellect. The same happens when some people irritate you. Observe that irritation. What happens? You get irritated, but somehow you manage to suppress. And the next time and the next time...the more you suppress your irritation, one day you just blow it all off. It all becomes so unbearable, it comes flooding out. Don't keep such a company.

You know, you always keep the company of someone who is similar to you, or who you think is on your wave length, or equal to you. When someone is above you, you honour him, you respect him, idolize him. When someone is below you, then you don't bother to take any notice of him, you brush him off. The company that you long for, or you want to keep, is that which is on par with you. And that is where all the anger and frustration start arising out of you. Either you become very small and keep everything above you or you become so big and see everything as insignificant, everything as that which doesn't matter at all - then you feel much more freedom.

Kastarati, kastarati mayam? Yah sangah tyajati, yo mahanubhavam sevate, nirmamo bhavati

Kastarati, kastarati mayam? Who crosses this ocean of illusion, this ocean of unreality? One who shuns the company - *yah sangah tyajati.*

You label yourself, "I am somebody, I am something, I am this, I am that, I am like this. I am an angry person." You have labelled yourself and you justify yourself being an angry person because you have labelled yourself, and you feel happy being angry all the time.

You have to take off all of your labels.

You know, you really do not know who you are. Sometimes if you enter into somebody's kitchen, the labels tell you something, but there is something else in the bottle. The container contains something else, the label says something else. And that is exactly what you are! You are labeling yourself as somebody, but inside you, you are something completely different. Take off your labels!

Yo mahanubhavam sevate, nirmamo bhavati - one who serves the Enlightened, one who serves the wise, one who keeps wise company, becomes free from this feeling of "I want this, I want that, I, I, I." You exist as though you do not, you live as though you do not. Hollow and empty - you exist like a feather. You have no demands. You don't demand that people need to recognize you. So what if everyone doesn't recognize you, or if everyone recognizes you, so what? Let the whole world recognize you, so what? And if

64

nobody recognizes you, so what? There are flowers in the garden, there are flowers in the forest. Do they say, "Oh, nobody saw me, I have blossomed?" Does it matter to the rose whether someone looks at it or not? In fact, if people look at it, they may pluck it! It is better nobody sees them - they are happy.

This urge for recognition from somebody is what kills you. You do your job and that's it! What has to come to you, will come to you. Why do we need to crave for other's recognition? That brings ego - "Me, me, me, I did it." So many lives like this you have existed on this planet and they have all gone - so many mosquitoes like you.

You know that story of an elephant and the fly on it's leg? A fly was living on the leg of an elephant. Once the fly got so angry at the elephant, it said, "I am leaving you today! Finished! Enough is enough! I'm done with you." It got so angry, it left. At that moment, just by accident, the elephant moved it's leg and some dust arose. But the fly thought that the storm has come because it is leaving the elephant. It told the elephant, "Yes, you see, the storm has come? I am leaving you - you suffer from the storm." The elephant didn't even know that the fly was sitting on its leg! And that is how nobody really cares what you are, what you do, what you don't do. And all impact gets wiped out by the flood of time. Time comes and just floods you, wipes you out, wipes all the memory out of this planet. This *me, me, me* can only dissolve and you serve. *Nirmano bhavati* - he becomes free from this identity of ego, identity of the smallness. Identifying yourself with the smallness...because this smallness is the cause of misery. "I was not recognized. Nobody looked at me, nobody loves me." Come on, wake up. You ARE love!

Love is in giving, not in demanding.

Recognize how much love there is for you. The air loves you, that is why it is getting into your nose and coming out of it! The earth loves you, that is why it is holding on to you with it's gravitational force, otherwise you would have become like a helium balloon - crying and yelling, going up, up - or your head would be sticking to the ceiling. The day the earth stops loving you, just imagine, what would happen if the earth loses it's gravitational force for you? You will cry, "Hey, hold me!" The sun loves you, that is why the sun shines on you. This entire creation is filled with love.

But this little foolish mind says *"Me, Me, I, I, I did this, I did that, I want this, I want that, I like this, I don't like this"*. This identity is what suffocates you, what limits your potential. You are much more than what you think you are. You are so vast, you are so great! And this little dust in your eyes makes you unable to see the vastness that you are. This little dust that gets into your eyes prevents you from seeing the vastness of the sky.

Yo viviktasthanam sevate, yo lokabandha munmulyati, nistraygunyo bhavati, yogakshemam tyajati

Who becomes free? He is talking about those who become free. Freedom is a necessity. Politicians say freedom is your birthright. I don't say it is your right. I say freedom is your necessity, your need - it is not a right. You cannot live without freedom. And the spiritual path is not that which makes you more bonded, it releases all the bondage and makes you free. The goal of a spiritual path is to bring you freedom, which is the need of every soul. That is why we come to this planet - to be free. *Yo viviktasthanam sevate* - one who reposes in that corner deep inside oneself, where there is nothing else. One who is alone, who sits alone, can never feel lonely. If you cannot be alone, then you will start feeling lonely. *Viviktasthanam* means where there is nobody else. That doesn't mean you run to the forest. You may even be sitting in a forest, or alone in a desert, but your mind will be filled with all the things and events and people. No. When you can settle into that space where there is nobody, when you become hollow and empty, you can be free. And get into that place again and again. *Sevate* - who enjoys being alone, one who is not worried about what people tell them or talk about them.

Yo lokabandha munmulyati - one who is not worried about what people tell them or talk about them can be free. You don't worry about what people think about you. They may think good about you, they may think bad about you. Why sit and worry all the time about what others think about you? It may not be true at all! *Lokabandha munmulyati* - one who is free from this bondage of the surroundings, of society.

Yo yogakshemam tyajati - and one who is beyond all the three gunas - the satva, rajas and tamas. *Satva guna* - knowledge, *Rajo guna* - desire, ambition, restlessness and *Tamo guna* - dullness and sleep. The three gunas bring different tendencies in you and you are not attached to any one of them. Know that it is easy to be detached from negative qualities, but you get attached to positive qualities. You think you are the only righteous person and then you get upset about everybody else who is not righteous. Feeling that you are the only right one, the only honest one, the only correct person, others, naturally, become bad. That is attachment to the positive qualities. One needs to be free from attachment to the positive qualities, also. Then you will really be free.

Yo yogakshemam tyajati - one who is free from acquiring and maintaining whatever has come in life. There are two worries - one is to get what one doesn't have and the other is to maintain what one has. These two worries eat you up! And one who does not worry about them, really crosses this ocean of misery, of maya.

67

Om Namoh Bhagavate Vasudevaya
Om Namoh Bhagavate Vasudevaya
Om Namoh Bhagavate Vasudevaya

Who brought the ocean of conflict in life? Narada says,

Yo viviktasthanam sevate, yo lokabandha munmulyati, nistraygunyo bhavati, yogakshemam tyajati - one who is not after attaining what he does not have, achieving what he has not achieved, is not feverish about holding on to what he has. One who is free, light, easy. In the next sutra, he explains :

Yat karmaphalam tyajati, karmani sanyasyati, tato nirdvando bhavati

When we act, behind every action there is a motivation. And the motivation is to get a specific result. There is no action that we do intentionally without an eye on a specific goal. That achievement affects our process of action. Are you getting what I am saying? Okay, let us see it from this angle. There are some actions which you do as an expression of joy in which you are not bothered about the result of the action. There are some other actions which you do expecting to get a certain result out of it, a joy out of it. The *expectation of joy* in an action makes the action inferior. But an action which happens as an *expression of joy* has no fruit of action, no result that you are looking for. When you are happy, you want to spread that happiness, and if you are keenly observing whether the other person has become happy or not, you get entangled in their vicious circle. *Yat karmaphalam tyajati* - when you are in conflict, what can you do? There is a Chinese saying, " Take a pillow and go to bed." Narada says a similar thing, with a little difference. He says you rest. Take a break from the action. Take a break from the activity. Not just the activity, but the fruit of the activity, the result of the activity. The concern about the outcome of your activity is what pulls you down, what bothers you. Suppose you want to take up a project, want to do some work. Now whether it will happen or not, if you start putting your mind on all these concerns, then your whole enthusiasm gets dampened. When you are aware of your potential and you want to do an action, just jump into it. Go into it, is what Narada says, without having a concern about the outcome.

Karmani sanyasyati - be so centred in the action. Relax, let go of the action. When you are in conflict, any activity you do, you will be in a bigger conflict. When you have a choice in front of you and you choose one, you will always find the other side is greener. The other choice seems much better. This thing will bother you, will not let you enjoy what you have in your hand, not let you focus on what is right now in your hand. So when you are bothered by a choice, relax. The choice is never between good and bad. There is no choice between pudding and a plate of clay. The choice is between whether you should have pudding or apple pie. Never mind, today you have apple pie and tomorrow you have a pudding. So what? Your confusion is always about bad and worse or good and better. The conflict is because of the choice. Narada says relax. You can have conflict throughout your life - from choosing what subject you want to select in your school to what job you should do and which partner you should have as a life partner. There is ample amount of choice. One woman came to me for blessings saying, "Guruji, I am going shopping today, please bless me. I always do the wrong shopping. I buy the wrong saris, the wrong garments. Then I come back home, again I have to go back. So please bless me that I make the right selection." Our childish mentality has not gone. Just like children you know - you take them to *Toys 'r 'us* and they don't want to go back home. Either they want to take the whole shop home or they choose one toy and then they get confused. And they end up crying in the end. Choices are what bring conflict in your life, that enhance the conflict in life. Where there is conflict, there is no love. How can you be centred when there is conflict? And how to be centred? He says relax.

Karmani sanyasyati - one who can just *let go* of that. But that doesn't mean he does not act. In the previous sutra he said though one who is wise, who has attained knowledge, Divine love is beyond all action, he continues to engage himself in action.

Bhavatu nishchay dadhyadupam shastrarakshana - to maintain a discipline, maintain the shastras, the scriptures. One still follows them, though one is above all that.

Yat karmaphalam tyajati, karmani sanyasyati - one who is not concerned about the outcome of an action, one who is centred while in action, and one who reposes in the self - he goes beyond the dualities, beyond the conflicts.

Tato nirdvando bhavati - one who even rises beyond the vedas, beyond the knowledge, he attains the pure love.

Yo vedanapi sanyasyati, kevalam avichinn anuragam labhate

Vedas means injunctions. "Do this, you have to do this" - laws and rules and regulations for the betterment of oneself, one's society, one's environment. This is one meaning of the vedas. Another meaning of *ved* means knowledge. One who goes even beyond the vedas. That is why it is called vedanta - where knowledge ends. Going beyond knowledge. You know a student wants to gain knowledge, but a devotee doesn't care for knowledge. He just loves, that is all. Love is beyond knowledge. That is the difference between a student and a devotee. A student's goal is to gain some knowledge, gain something out of it. But a devotee, a beloved is one who simply loves. When there is love, you don't need to know anything about any of it. Like a child is not interested in knowing how the mother is, isn't it? A child can never make the mother an object of knowing. A child never gets curious about the mother.

Knowing is a curiosity, love is uniting.

Knowing is analysis, love is synthesis.

One who is beyond analysis, one who doesn't sit all the time doubting "Oh what is he up to, what is she up to, who is there, what is that...?" is simply in love. Love is having a sense of oneness, belongingness. Same with the mother. However the child is, it is part of her. A mother never becomes curious about the child. "What does my son thinks about me, what does my daughter think about me," she does not sit and worry. You must cultivate this in your relationship.

Often newly married couples become too curious about each other - they try to dig each other's history and each other's background, each other's activities. And in this analysis they become separate. Doubts come, problems come, mistrust comes and they blame each other. You know, in rural society in India, this is not a question. Once someone is married , there is synthesis. They take each other for granted, they don't question each others integrity or any such thing. There is synthesis there. Ofcourse, in today's society it is turning around. East is no more east, west is no more west. Even in the eastern part of the globe cities are almost like in the west. And in the west, values are turning back. Family emphasis is growing much more than what it was a couple of decades ago.

You cannot understand love through your intellect. It is something to be felt. And anything that needs to be felt, needs synthesis, not analysis. You have to become one with it to know it.

Someone asked, "How to know Brahman, how to know God?".

71

It is said you have to become Brahman in order to know Brahman. Or knowing which you become *That*. And how do you know? Not through the head. Because whatever you know through the head, you always keep at a distance. You are separate. The subject-object difference will remain. But feeling is not that way, love is not like that. Love is the knowledge that comes out of synthesis. The taste of the pudding is in tasting, music is in hearing it. In the same way, feeling. If you know Brahman, you have become Brahman. Synthesis is the language of love. And for that you need to transcend knowledge, the analytical aspect of life.

Yo vedanapi sanyasyati - and you can only transcend what you have gone through, you can only leave what you have. If you say leave the fruit of action means if you never act, you never have a fruit of action to leave. How can you leave something which you don't have? This is so beautiful. Dropping the attachment to the fruit of action means if you have never acted, how can you drop the action or the fruit of action? So be active. Keep doing your work, and drop the fruit of action. When you have to act, in the beginning you have to be motivated. All the fruit of action is kept in front of you. Krishna did the same to Arjuna. He told him that if you die, you will attain heaven and if you win, you will rule over the world, you will be an Emperor. "Come on fight." He tells him the fruit of the action. Jesus also kept the fruit of action in front so that a lazy goose could finally start.If you are bogged with *tamo guna*, laziness, you need motivation to do something and the fruit of action, *result,* is a motivating factor. When you are shown the result you will get, you start acting. When you are acting then you say drop the result. Just work. These are the ways of the wise to take step by step. You can't tell them see you said all lies. Before you said you get, now you say drop .....no. Truth is contradictory, truth is multidimensional. Truth cannot be comprehended on a linear thinking. You need a spherical thinking, global thinking.

is contradictory, truth is multidimensional. Truth cannot be comprehended on a linear thinking. You need a spherical thinking, a global thinking. *Yo vedanapi sanyasyati, kevalam avichinn anuragam labhate* - the One who has transcended knowledge, who has transcended action, who has gone beyond the action and knowledge *kevalam avichina* - he attains that pure love which is everlasting, which never leaves you or breaks you, which never gets distorted or dissipated.

Sa tarati, sa tarati, sa lokam sa taryati

He alone crosses this ocean of sansara, maya. He alone crosses. *Sa lokam, sa taryati* - he can redeem the world. He alone can take up any amount of stress from anybody and then dissolve it. He can redeem the whole world, uplift the whole world. That much patience, power and wisdom he gains. And he alone can do.

In the scriptures they say there are five signs of a Sadguru -
Gyana raksha - in the presence of a Master, wisdom and knowledge is protected. You move away from the wise person and you seem to lose your knowledge, you seem to forget. But in the presence of the Master, all the knowledge comes up. There is protection of knowledge, of wisdom, for generations to come.

Dukhakshaya - sorrow diminishes.

Sukhavirbhava - for no apparent reason joy wells up, happiness comes to you.

Sarvasamvardhana - all talents blossom, hidden talents in people come up. Those who cannot sing, start singing, those who cannot write, start writing poems. Those who cannot cook, start cooking very well. People who could never speak in front of people start speaking. All the talents that are hidden in you, come up in you.

Samridhi - everything is in plenty, there is no dearth of anything.

These are the five signs you see around a Sadguru - everything is full. *Sa tarati sa tarati, sa lokam sa taryati.* And he can redeem the world of its misery.

Love is Beyond Proof

Anirvachaniyam premswaroopam

Mookaswaadanvat

Prakaashte kvapi patre

Gunrahitam kamanarahitam pratikshana vardhamaanam
avichinnam sukshmataram anubhavarupam

Tat praapya tadeva avlokyati, tadeva shrunoti, tadeva
bhashyati, tadeva chintayati

Gauni tridha gunabhedaat, aartaadi bhedaat va

Uttarsmaad uttarsmaat poorva poorva shreyaya bhavati

Anayasmat saulabhayam bhaktau

Pramaan antarasya annapekshatvat svayam pramanatvat

Shantirupaat paramananda rupascha

Loka hanau chinta na karya, niveditatma lokaveda tvat

Na tadsidhau lokavyavaharo heyah,
kintu phaltyaagah tatsadhanam cha karyameva

Om Namoh Bhagavate Vasudevaya
Om Namoh Bhagavate Vasudevaya
Om Namoh Bhagavate Vasudevaya

Throughout the ages, with all gestures, man is trying to express love - but it has remained inexpressible. Love is so deep somewhere in you, and you find all your expressions just a shadow of it. Often teenagers say that nobody understands them - it is a normal complaint. Just remember when you were a teenager, what was your complaint? "Nobody understands me!" isn't that so? Nobody understands you or you find yourself incapable of expressing what you feel? If the feeling is so superficial, then it can be expressed. But the feeling that is so genuine, so deep, so authentic, is hard to express.

That is what Narada says in the next sutra :

Anirvachaniyam premswarupam

*Anirvachaniyam - **cannot** be expressed!* That is the nature of love! Tears will come, a glow comes on your face, the smile comes up. But words fail to express.

Often all these outer expressions give you a *glimpse* of love, but not really the *experience* of it.

Anirvachaniyam premswarupam - cannot be expressed by words. Language is of the mind, of intellect. You can express any theory, theorem, philosophy through words. But feelings can only be

74

felt. Communication on that level is beyond speech. And when lovers speak, they don't make much sense.

Mukaswadanvat

Like when a dumb person tastes something great, how does he say that? *Mukaswadanvat* - like the taste of a dumb person, like the joy of one who cannot speak! Those who have eyes can see, those who have hearts can feel. Love is what you *are*! Love is that energy which is the basis of this whole creation. How can that be confined to a few words that we blabber through our mouth?

Forget about it, if you think you are just going to understand love through words. You expect people to tell you, "I love you! I love you!" and all such phrases. Many times you say, "I love you" but it doesn't really carry that feeling, that energy behind it. Such words go in vain. *Mukaswadanvat* - like a dumb person, be silent!

When two people are in love, there is a demand that arises between them. Let the other *Tell* me something more! And however many words you hear, it is not enough - still you feel inadequate! "Today you didn't talk to me. Why you didn't talk to me? You don't love me...!"

Om Namoh Bhagavate Vasudevaya
Om Namoh Bhagavate Vasudevaya
Om Namoh Bhagavate Vasudevaya

Mukaswadanvat - love is like the taste of a dumb person. A dumb person who can taste but cannot express in words how wonderful the food is.

Prakashate kvapi patre

Such intense love for the Divine shines through here and there, somewhere and sometimes. Every human being is nothing but a vessel to hold the consciousness. There is no difference between me and you and you and him and him and her. We are all just empty bowls. Everyone is nothing but an empty bowl, and the same space is in all the bowls. In ancient India, the example of the earthen pot was given. The body is like an earthen pot and the soul is contained in the earthen pot as an individual soul. The moment the pot is broken, the space remains in space. Nothing has happened to the space. We are all pots. Every living creature is a pot. But such Divine love shines though only in some pots.

Prakashate kvapi patre - not that it is not there. But it shines through in some pots. It is present everywhere, in all pots. But it only shines through, manifests somewhere here and there, on a rare occasion, once in thousands of years, once in a few centuries. Such deep Divine love shines through, so that all other pots also can get inspired to shine that same love - *prakashate kvapi patre*.

*Gunarahitam kamanarahitam pratikshanavardhamanam
avichinnam sukshmataram anubhavarupam*

Gunarahitam - it is free from the three types of different love.
There are three types of love - *Satvik* love is unconditional love. I
love you for what you are, not because you did something for me.
You helped me so much, so I love you - this *Rajasik* love is the
second type of love. I love you because you did this for me. *Tamasik*
love is the third type of love. Tamasik love is love because we have
a common enemy -"I don't like that person. Oh, you also do not like
that person? Come we are friends, we love each other."

The first category of love is - "I love you because the way you
are is simply lovable. What you did to me is not a matter of concern
at all." "Because you give me some pleasure, because you helped
me, because you care for me, I love you," is Rajasik love. There is a
string attached to Rajasik love. Loving because you hate somebody
else is Tamasik love. Making friends to gain strength to hate is Tamasik
love. Do you see what I am saying? Often two people get together
just because they have a common enemy. Their common goal is to
eliminate or destroy something, so they get together. That bonding
out of ignorance, out of dullness or destruction is Tamasik love.

Divine love is beyond - it transcends all these three types of
love.

Gunrahitam kamanarahitam - there are no strings attached
in that love. "If you love me, I love you; if you do this thing to me, I
love you. If you are nice to me, then I love you." How about if I am
not nice to you, would you still love me? No question. You see?
These conditional strings are attached to your expression of feelings
of love. This is *kamanasahitam*. Divine love is *kamanarahitam* -
is devoid of any strings, any desires, any conditions.

Pratikshamane vardamanam - it grows moment by moment,

it does not diminish. Often in our relationships love seems to diminish. At least the intensity goes down a little, in all relationships - when a child is very small, it cannot move away from it's mother even for a few minutes, a few hours. Then it starts becoming independent. Then once in a while the child sends Mother's Day cards. You are more attached to your children than to your own parents. Your whole attention, that was so much with your parents when you were a child, gets diverted to your spouse after you get married. Then after you have children, that same attention you had for spouse gets diverted to your children. There is a shifting in all different types of love. But Divine love grows all the time, moment by moment. *Pratikshanam vardamanam* - every moment it grows, it increases, never decreases.

Avichinnam - there is no gap. It cannot be destroyed by anybody, it cannot be taken away from you. *Sukshmataram* - and it is very delicate. To experience it you need to be very quiet. Love itself is so delicate. That is why when you feel love, you feel so delicate, so vulnerable. And that is how you can get hurt. Hurt is part of love. When you love somebody, you feel so delicate, so vulnerable. And a small simple gesture from them hurts you. When one whom you love does not smile at you, finished, your mood is off. Small gestures, insignificant things can hurt you - because love is so delicate

Sukshmataram - finer than the finest. It is said that to know God, you need to be in love. Why should you be in love in order to know God? Because love makes you very fine, refined, so delicate. In that delicate state of consciousness alone can you be united with this whole Universe. Then you can say, "Me and my father are one." Unless you are in that state of love, you cannot proclaim, "Me and my father are one," you cannot say *"Aham Brahmasmi"* - *I am that*. When can you say it? When your consciousness becomes so refined. From the molecular state to the atomic level to the sub-atomic level - then you can say there is one field. On the gross level you cannot say 'one field'. Only on the subtle level you can recognize there is one field - the oneness in creation.

Anubhavrupam - it is experiential, not an intellectual analysis. It is a synthesis of the finest order. It is not the cloud which is there one day and which breaks another day, with some conditions, with some feelings. People often fall in love and then say they got disillusioned. That is really no disillusionment, it is *re-illusionment.*

If you break away from love and fall into a state of apathy or negativity or dullness, it is not disillusionment. Disillusionment is when you completely immerse yourself in love and you recognize there is only one love in this universe. Then you are disillusioned. (Laughter) Real disillusionment is when you realize the sun belongs to you, when you realize this whole planet is your own and you own the air you breathe. That is disillusionment. Otherwise you are an illusion. Small identity is what is your illusion. *Me, mine, my thing.* This experiential Divine love brings you the reality. But it is so strange that when people fall out of love, that is when they say, "I got disillusioned." When they become indifferent, they say they are disillusioned. That is small mindedness, small love. Then they have not had a taste of what Divine love is.

Tat prapya tadeva avlokyati, tadeva shrunoti, tadeva bhashyati, tadeva chintayati

Attaining which you are compelled to talk about it all the time. You only think about it and nothing else. And you see only that everywhere - the impact of that love is so strong.

Tadeva bhashyati tadeva chintayati - you see only that everywhere. Your world is your own projection, your own creation. When you feel negative, you see all that negativity in everybody. If you are upset, you feel everybody is upset with you - the world is a hopeless place for you. When you feel down, you feel everything is hopeless, isn't it so? When you are high with energy and enthusiasm, nothing matters to you, you just move, you feel you can move the world, isn't it? When you are in love you only see that.

Tadeva bhashyati - you only speak about it, you only immerse in it. Every particle of Divine love! And that is what is worth attaining.

Om Namoh Bhagavate Vasudevaya
Om Namoh Bhagavate Vasudevaya
Om Namoh Bhagavate Vasudevaya

There is a proverb that says, "The world is as you see it." If you feel good in you, then you see good everywhere. If your mind is bitter, you see everything is bitter. *Yatha drishti, tatha srishti* - the world is as your vision.

A hungry man looks at the moon, he only sees it like a doughnut or it reminds him of a bagel! Someone who is in a new love affair, he looks at the moon and it reminds him of his beloved's face.

If you feel negative, then you see everything as negative. Often when people get sick, they feel everybody is falling sick. They telephone and talk to a few people and they are also sick! In a town of a million people, they might have spoken to ten, fifteen, twenty people, most of them are sick and then they conclude everybody is sick.

We generalize, eternalize the problem. Sometimes when you are upset you say, "I've always been like this," don't you? But if you have always been upset, you will never even notice that you are upset! For you to be miserable, you should have some gaps of happiness, some relief somewhere. (Laughter) If you are in a continuous state of misery, you cannot know misery at all, you cannot even feel it. But the mind usually generalizes the problem and eternalizes it, "It is always like this, I'm always doing mistakes." If you are always doing mistakes, that won't be a mistake. That is how you are! That is your nature. And nature is never a mistake! Nature is nature, it is not a mistake at all.

If everything is wrong, remember something is basically wrong with you. Not everything can be wrong, not everybody can be wrong. As is your vision, so is your creation. Set right the vision. If the vision is to the Divine, the Divinity deepens. Then you see the Divine everywhere.

That is the next sutra that Narada says -

Tat prapya tadeva avalokyati, tadeva shrunoti, tadeva bhashyati, tadeva chintyati

Having attained that love, that Divine love, one sees only that everywhere. *Tadeva avalokyati* - they cannot but see only love. Even if someone is blaming you, you see some good in it. "See this person is pointing that out, it is good." You don't see blame as blame. You see that blame as an effort from that person to point out a mistake, which nobody dares to point out, or at the most, you see they are taking away some bad karma of yours.

It is said if someone blames you for no reason, you should thank them twice. If anyone blames you, they are taking the bad karma away from you. Someone who praises you, they are taking the good karma away from you! Now you choose what you want! So someone praises you, better praise back immediately. (Laughter) But when someone blames you, better keep quiet, otherwise you may take more bad karma from them - they may have bigger stock than you, bigger stuff, heavier duty than you! (Laughter)

Tat prapya tadeva avalokyati - you see only that perfection. When you attain perfection, you see only perfection. *Tadeva shrunoti* - and you would like to listen only to that, "Tell me more about love, tell me more about what is the secret, the mystery of this universe." Otherwise inquisitiveness is always about something that is negative, some scandal, "Oh, tell me what it is! What happened? I would like to hear from you what happened." Gossip is most of the time about scandals, because that is what you nurture. You seem to enjoy it. But attaining Divine love, that is not what you are interested in. You are interested in knowing more about love, more about the leelas, more about the happiness. "Tell me more what has happened, tell me more, what more new knowledge has come today?" This interest in knowledge, interest in the mystery of the universe, interest in listening to the glory, is what you come up with - not the complaints, not the problems, not the unhappiness, not the wrong happenings, not the imperfections. Interest in imperfection is a sign of sickness.

Tadeva shrunoti - even if someone calls you 'ghost', you will hear mentioned Holy Ghost! You would like to hear the best from them. When people go to talks and lectures, you ask them afterwards, "What did you hear?" and you will be surprised! They will pick up some negative things here and there, "Oh, this is what I heard." This indicates the interest in negativity of the mind. This interest in negative things indicates the stress level of the mind, the smallness of the mind, how one is not yet open to the ocean of love that one *is - tadeva shrunoti.*

Tadeva bhashyati - you only talk about it, talk about that alone. *Tadeva chintyati* - think about that alone. You dwell, you read, just think about that, you are in awe every moment.

Gauni tridha gunabhedat, aarta adi bhedat va

This is unconditional love. This is the love that is beyond all characteristics, beyond all the gunas, beyond all conditions. But lesser than this is the three types of love, that is, the satvik, rajasik and tamasik love, as we already heard.

There are four types of people who pray to God. In the world you can categorize four types of people:

First is *aarta* - one who is miserable, one who has problems nobody else can solve - no doctors can, nobody can do anything about you, then you pray to God. *Aarta* - those who are miserable, they pray to God.

Then *artharti* - the second type of people who pray to God are those who want something, some gains, some material benefits, or whatever, satisfaction. You will see just before the exams, students go to places of worship and pray - just before exams or just before results come out! Or if they have to go to an interview, people pray. Sometimes even for lottery tickets! While buying a lottery ticket people pray and say, "If I get the lottery, 10% I will give to you, God!" *Artharti* - if you go to shops, retail shops, even wholesale shops, they all have altars. And there they worship, they pray that the business should be very good, that they have more profits or benefits - *artharti*.

And *jigyasu*, the third category of people, who are inquisitive, who want to know whether there is a God, or *what is it*? And they are also in a prayerful mood - seekers, spiritual seekers. They don't want anything material, but they want something. A space in heaven - to the right side or left side or wherever… Enlightenment, praying for something, but they are not clear what it is. That is *jigyasu*, one who is aiming at something. But they don't know what it is. It is nothing tangible. They are neither miserable nor do they want anything material, they do not know what they want, but they want something! They are called *jigyasu*, the seekers.

And then *gyani* - means the enlightened, the knowledgable ones, those who have attained wisdom, they also pray. 'Pray' not in the sense we think about - "Oh God, give me this, give me that," no, no! Pray - commune; the wise commune with the Divine. They just know the Divinity is their very nature.

So, the four types of people and the three types of love - satvik, rajasik and tamasik. Tamasik love is when you love somebody because you both have common enemies. You love someone because they will help you to fight your enemy. Or the love of terrorists... you know terrorists have got a deep love for their cause, but their love is mixed with hatred. They are ready to give up their life for the cause. The cause may be very foolish, but for that cause they are ready to kill anybody or kill themselves. Their love for the cause is so strong And they are so stressed out. This is the tamasik love.

Rajasik love is the barter system. "If you love me, I'll love you. If you smile at me, I'll smile back at you. If you do this thing to me, if you are nice to me, then I'll be nice to you." This type of conditional love, or conditioned response, is rajasik love. In rajasik love you're either very high or very low. You get high one moment, the next moment you're down. You are excited, very happy, you jump up and down, and then you are completely down. One moment you are full of enthusiasm, next moment you are depressed. This is rajasik love.

And then satvik love. Satvik love is unconditional love. "I don't care what you do to me, but from my side I'm just going to love you. I love because I have no choice. I can't *but*, because I am love." This understanding, this tendency that arises from within you, that is satvik love.

From time to time, according to these four different categories of people, these three different types of love manifest in this world. And they can change also. You might have been in tamasik love ten years back, then you could have come to rajasik, and might have become satvik also. Wisdom brings you more and more into the satvik type of love.

Uttarsmaad uttarsmaat poorva poorva shreyaya bhavati

I explained in the reverse order. He says earlier is always better. Means satvik is better than rajasik, rajasik is better than tamasik. We spoke in the reverse direction - it is same thing.

Satvik is better than rajasik and rajasik is better than tamasik love. Similarly the knowledge, the wisdom, the love of a wise person, of a *gyani*, of an Enlightened, is better than that of a seeker. And a seeker's love is better than that of one who is craving for some material wealth, who is in pursuit of gaining something. And that is better than those who are miserable. Because a person who is miserable cannot hear! The eyes are blocked, they just speak. Someone who is in pursuit of some material comfort, his ears are a little more open, but open only to the subject which he wants. But a seeker, a spiritual seeker, his eyes and ears are much more open. And a *gyani* listens to this creation, he listens to silence, he listens to the unspoken words.

Any amount of advice or speech given to a miserable person is in vain, because they don't listen to you, isn't that your experience? If someone is miserable, if you give advice, does he hear you, listen to you? They are just closed. They have a one track mind, everything just goes above the head.

Uttarsmad uttarsmat - the satvik type of love is better. They all say the same. *Uttarsmad uttarsmat purva purva shreyaya bhavati* - the earlier one is better than the later one.

Anayasmat saulabhyam bhaktau

The question is how to get it, how to have it? This is the easiest path. Love is not a practice. It is just an acknowledgement. You only have to wake up and feel the sense of belongingness. Whether you do it today, after ten years, after ten lifetimes, it is up to you. But it doesn't take any time at all.

There is a proverb that says, "It may take some time to pluck a flower from a plant, or even to blink your eye, but it won't take any time to attain Divine love at all. It is instantaneous. *Anayasmat saulabhyam* - it is so easy, the easiest thing. Don't sit and wait to have a sense of belongingness sometime in the future. You are thoroughly mistaken. If you don't have a sense of belongingness today, you think it will come after ten years, after five years of doing asanas, pranayama and everything? Forget about it! It is the easiest thing.

Praman antarasya anapekshatvat svayam pramantvat

It means you don't need any other proof. Love, itself, is the proof. You don't have to go and ask someone, "Do I have love in my heart?" Nobody needs to authenticate you. Your knowledge needs an authentication, whether it is correct or not.

Your knowledge needs verification, whether it is authentic or not. Whether your perception is correct or not needs to be told to you by somebody. Your experience has to be told by someone - whether it is right or not.

But love is a proof in itself. *Svayam pramantvat* - it is the proof in itself. Just look into someone's eyes - you see whether they are worried or they are in love. In worry there is apathy… and in love you can see the spark in their eyes. When you can notice that in others, you think one cannot notice for oneself what is happening inside? It is impossible. It is like a pain in the neck or in the leg or in your stomach - anywhere you have a pain, can you not know it? Do you need someone else to prove that you have a pain? *Svayam pramantvat* - you know it, you feel it. It is instantaneous. No external proof is needed for such a love.

Shanti rupat paramananda rupascha

Two more attributes of Divine love, Narada explains : *shanti rupat* - the Divine love is of the nature of peace. And *Paramanand rupascha* - extreme bliss, extreme ecstasy. *Shantirupat* - peaceful. It is not the love of excitement - it is the love that comes with peace.

Usually love is associated with feverishness or excitement, tension, because you are in love, and you are worried whether the person whom you are in love with loves you or not. All the time there is the doubt, "Oh, I love that person so much, does he or she love me also or not? And what do they think?" Fear of losing that love! All these anxieties, feverishness distort love. But Divine love is *shantirupat*, there is such a serene calmness and peace with it. *Paramanandarupascha* - there is inexpressible joy, bliss.

Loka hanau chinta na karya, niveditatma lokaveda sheeltvat

A glimpse of such love doesn't take time, of course, that is true. But to stabilize that love, to maintain it in our daily life, it needs some strength, it needs some time. *Loka hanau chinta na* - what to do? If your world is crumbling around you, don't worry about it, because you have surrendered, you have offered everything to the Divine; *niveditatma* - yourself, the world, your own world. When you belong to the Divine, you think your world doesn't belong to the Divine? When you belong to the Divine, your family also belongs to the Divine, your whole world belongs to the Divine, your knowledge belongs to the Divine, your character belongs to the Divine.

Niveditatma lokaveda sheeltvat - we are worried about ourselves, we are worried about our family, about our reputation, about our knowledge, our correctness or incorrectness of the knowledge. These are the four main principles that cause worry to you. You worry about what people think about you, you worry about how you can carry on your life. Don't worry, when you have offered yourself to the Divine, all this also belongs to the Divine. So you don't have to worry, nature will take care of it, the Divine will take care of it.

There is a story of Draupadi. She was asking for help from Krishna. But with one hand she was holding herself. She was a queen of Arjuna and she was stripped in an open assembly by the king of that place. She was holding the sari in one hand and she was calling for help from the other. She never got the help. But when she had to leave both hands and with both her hands up she cried, then the help came; then the sari, the cloth that she was wearing would never finish. The more he stripped, the more it would grow. Have you heard this story? And he got tired, because the pile of sari came up high, and his hands were so tired stripping it off her. But he could not succeed. This is one of the stories about how Draupadi threw both her hands up and cried for help.

There is another story about Krishna. Once He had sat down to eat, persons were serving him… He was eating the food when he suddenly got up in the middle of the meal and ran, saying, "My devotee is in trouble." Everyone kept saying, "Oh, no, don't go, eat the food and then go!" He went to the door - and then He came back. He said, "He was calling me, but then he took care of himself." There are many stories, many events in your own life when you were really desperate and when you dropped all your hang-ups - the help definitely came. But if you are holding onto a handle with one hand and then trying to jump, it is like holding onto the diving board and wanting to swim. You are neither in the water nor are you on the diving board! You are hanging somewhere in-between.

Loka hanau chinta na karya - if it appears that you are losing, everything is going haywire, don't worry about losing anything. *Niveditatma lokaveda sheeltvat* - because you have offered all this, it is already done.

Na tad sidhau loka vyavharo heyah
kintu phaltyagah tatsadhanam cha karyameva

Until that perfection is achieved, even before the result appears, keep acting. Keep acting, but don't worry about the fruit of action. Don't be attached to the result of an action. Don't think you are in control of everything. This is the greatest illusion! You know, success brings more illusion, because when you are successful, you think you achieved it. But if someone else repeats all that you did, I tell you, they won't be successful. This has happened. There is no prototype for success in the world; no, what do you call it ...? *Formula.* There is no concrete formula for success, I tell you. This could be a formula! One formula for success : there is no formula for success!

All these advertisements you see, how to make money, so and so did that... just go a little deeper into it. You will see it is emptier than it is full. It is all hype, isn't it? What do you say? You know, one gentleman was just an apple vendor in the street, and he made a huge amount of money, became a very successful person. You think every apple vendor can become so successful? You hear the story and then you think, "Okay, I can also sell apples on the street to become successful like that person!" It doesn't work like that. There is something called karma!

The rishi says that there is no doubt everything works and happens according to karma, but you don't just sit! Don't be feverish about the result. Just act with joy.

Tat sadhanam cha karyameva - yes, you heard, "Guruji said today there is no point in pranayama, meditation, why do all this, don't start! *Tat sadhanam cha.* Don't stop singing, don't stop meditating, all this, until you get perfectly grounded in the love. Until you are perfectly grounded in your centre, these things will have to be continued. And even after it becomes your nature, you will automatically sit and be in the state of meditation.

Tat sadhanam cha karyameva - he removes the steam out of the whole thing, out of the feverishness of expectation of your action. Then the action becomes more grounded. When you act with an expectation, you are ready to get frustrated and complain a little later. See, you have meditated for twenty years, "What did I get?" See what you got. You did not know that twenty years of meditation has made you a much better person. And after twenty years, one day you got upset and you say, "See twenty years of meditation, I still got upset, miserable!" You could have been miserable all the twenty years otherwise! You should say in spite of your meditation you got upset. Suppose you were never doing, what would have happened? You could have been much worse. None of the sadhanas or practices are to be left or shunned until you get centred. And they always improve you. We don't expect that one day in the future *I will experience, I will be in Divine love.* Right now it is paradoxical to listen to that. It doesn't take a second, yet, it will take some time! It is paradoxical. And truth is always paradoxical!

A Master and a disciple were going in a boat. Behind them there was a group of four people in another boat. These four were teasing the disciple who was going behind the Master. You know, usually if you follow some spiritual path, people who don't consider themselves to be spiritual, or consider themselves very *normal* people, consider you as abnormal - they make fun of you. So those boys were making fun of him, and sometimes even throwing things at him, torturing him. When they got into the boat, the boat with the four people capsized and started sinking. They had a very difficult time and barely managed to come to the shore alive.

The Master's boat with the disciple reached the shore safely, but because the other boat capsized and they were saved with great difficulty, the Master gave a slap to the disciple. You know why? He said, "Look, you should have spoken something back. You kept quiet. And if you had punished them, Nature wouldn't have punished them. You did not punish them, so Nature punished them even worse. Your patience made them suffer more." Look at the compassion of the Master. It is an event that happened, this is not just a story. It is such a great lesson. A person who is in equanimity and peace, even if he scolds, blames, it is taken as a blessing, something good is happening. (That doesn't happen very often.)

Don't drop all your practices. Stick to them until maturity comes. It is said that love and compassion for the whole creation, for all beings is the goal and you are the proof.

Question: Guruji, you said the compassion of the Master was shown by that slap? Could you explain why?

Guruji: Yes, he taught a lesson to the disciple. Upto a certain level in your knowledge, in your evolution, you have to be patient. When? When you have feverishness. And then compassion is born, equanimity, because you want to be calm, quiet, peaceful, patient for your own good, isn't it? But the Master's mind was thinking about the good of all the others, too. Do you get it?

Question: Yes. Did it also take away some karma from that boy?

Guruji: It taught him something, it lifted him to one more level. Until then he was thinking about his own behavior, the way to conduct himself, now he was given an understanding that you have to be compassionate. Get it? It is very subtle and very deep.

Merging with the Divine

Stridhan naastik vaira charitram na shravaniyam

Abhimana dambhadikam tyajyam

Tadarpitakhilacharah san kama krodha abhimanadika tasminneva karaneeyam

Trirupa bhanga purvakam nityadasya nityakanta bhajanatmakam prema karyam premaiva karyam

Bhakta ekantino mukhyah

Kantavarodha romanchashrubhih parasparam lapamanah pavayanthi kulani prithvim cha

Teerthikurvanthi teerthani, sukarmeekurvanthi karmani sachcha sthree kurvanthi shastrani

Tanmayah

Modante pitaro nrityanti devatah, sanatha cheyam bhurbhavati

Naasti teshu jaati vidya rupa kula dhana kriyadi bhedah

Yatstadiyah

Vado navalambyah

Bahulyavakashtvad aniya tatvaacha

Bhakthi shastrani mananiyani tadudbodhaka karmani karaneeyani

Sukha dukha ichcha labhadityakte kaale prateekshamane kshanardhamapi vyartham na neyam

Ahimsa satya shauch daya aastikyadi charitrayani paripalniyani

Om Namoh Bhagavate Vasudevaya
Om Namoh Bhagavate Vasudevaya
Om Namoh Bhagavate Vasudevaya

Two of the main channels for the mind to move outward are the sense of sight and hearing. What attracts you is what you hear about or what you see. When you have heard from someone that a particular movie is so nice, so good, your interest is kindled in that direction. You move in that direction. And similarly if you see something that attracts you, then you would like to hear more and more about it. Sight and hearing are the two that pull you outward. And, it happens, that most of the time obsessions come to us not through our own experience, but just by hearing about other peoples' experiences, or seeing others' experiences. Your mind is calm, serene, contented, happy, someone comes and says, "Look, look! You know you invest there and you will make so many millions! You have to invest only $10,000 dollars! You can make 230 million!" Your mind goes, "What? Okay, I want to do that!" And you also lose the $10,000! Greed comes to your mind, isn't it?

How much can you enjoy in life? There is a limit to enjoying, isn't it? Our senses are limited, but the greed, or what you have nurtured by hearing about from others, has created that hunger in you, thirst in you, which is difficult to quench. And the same with sex. You keep hearing about sex, seeing pornography... what is it? Pornography? All that thing. Then the mind gets entangled into it, into that feverishness, desire for it. These things pull the mind away

93

from the centre, then that calm, serene experience of deep love, of peace, is out of our sight. So, Narada says, the next Sutra:

Stridhan nastik vairy charitram na shravaniyam

Do not hear the glory or explanations of sex, money and atheism. A few years ago, rather a few decades ago, the atheists in India had only one argument to put forward. They used to say, "In Russia nobody believes in God, see how it is progressing? Why do we have to believe God? Russia is even better than America, an atheist country. They are enjoying, they are happy!" This was an illusion which was created by the media and publicity and all that. In India we used to get all these glorious books about the USSR, how glorious it is and how people were turning to Communism. Their whole philosophy was that all the past is rubbish. "Throw the whole past, it has no value - we have a golden future ahead." And what a golden future the USSR has seen. They were glorified, the atheists were glorified. "Why you have to know anything about Divine Love, why do you have to do any meditation, why do you have to serve, do anything at all? You can be better off." And you know, in the believers' mind also, that sowed the seed of doubt - "Oh, maybe there is no God. Maybe I am in a confusion. Maybe I should just go out and be merry, enjoy myself, and not worry about my evolution at all." When atheism is glorified, this type of getting back to the basic instinct, the animalistic tendency in human beings can destroy all the values, because values have no standing there. Isn't it?

And that is exactly what Narada says: *Stridhan nastik vairy charitram na shravaniyam* - if you keep thinking about sex all the time, your mind becomes so dull, gross. Not that sex is bad, but obsession about sex does not allow you to experience love. Because it is the same energy which is used as sex that becomes love, that is expressed as love also. *Stridhan nastik vairy charitram na*

94

shravaniyam - don't all the time sit and think about their glories, hear their glorification. That can tempt you. Someone says, "Hey, that would be better. You do this, become a millionaire - just do nothing." There is nothing wrong in becoming a millionaire. You can become a billionaire, no problem. But hearing about it creates a confusion, a feverishness, which is contrary to your blossoming. *Stridhan nastik vairy charitram na shravaniyam* - don't take an interest in listening to those things. •

Abhimandambhadikam tyajyam

Shun arrogance. You know, there can be two types of arrogance. There can be arrogance of renunciation also. "Look, I don't care, I am renounced. I don't want anything." That can be an arrogance, too. Arrogance of having and arrogance of not having, arrogance of intelligence, arrogance of service - "What do you think, I have done the maximum service. What do you think, who are you? What did you do? What service did you do? You are nothing!" - that type of attitude. Arrogance of service, arrogance of humility, arrogance of all your virtues, arrogance of being correct and having justice all the time. "I'm always right, I can never go wrong, I always do justice," that can create an arrogance in you. Drop this arrogance. Who are you? Wake up and see. Drop all your showing-off. All the "this is mine, mine and mine." What is yours? How long are you going to be on this planet? Wake up and see. *Abhimandambhadikam tyajyam* - drop this!

Tadarpitakhilacharah san kama krodha abhimanadika tasmineva karaneeyam

If you think it is not possible, it is not practical to live without a certain amount of pride, a certain amount of anger, or certain amount of lust, then say, "Do it all with the Divine only!" If you desire, desire the Divine! If you are passionate, be so passionate for the Divine. If

95

you are angry, be angry at the Divine! And if you are proud and arrogant, be proud, be arrogant that you own the owner of the creation, because you house Him in you, He is your prisoner. "The owner of this creation is my prisoner, he can't do anything without me." Have that pride, have that ego. If at all you think you cannot, just expand your everything. Because you offer everything to him.

Tadarpitakhilacharah san kama krodha abhimanadika tasmineva karaneeyam - whatever you want to be passionate about, just be passionate about everything in the Divinity. Pride? Take pride in it. You want to be greedy? Do Seva - be greedy about Seva, greedy about service. And you want to be angry? Be angry at the Divine. Tell Him, "Why don't you make more intelligent and bright people in creation. Don't you have better stock? You seem to be sometimes so dumb! You take away all intelligent people and give very long life to all the dumb people." If you want to be angry, just be angry at the Divine. Divert all your emotions to the Divine, yes?

Tadarpitakhilacharah san kama krodha abhimanadika tasminneva karaneeyam - you know, if you really want to worry, worry about what will happen after 5,000 years. Worry big. Expand everything. You will be comfortable. If you are just worrying about your knee problem, it becomes too much for you. But worry about the knee problems of all the people in this planet - find out how many people have knee problems. Must be several million people. Worry for this entire planet. Anything you do, when you expand it, you will find it is comfortable. Right from worry to anger to everything - it brings more awareness also.

Trirupa bhanga purvakam nitya dasya nityakanta bhajanatmakam prema karyam premaiva karyam

Whichever way you started - either satvik, rajsik or tamsik, or the three types of love - affection or love or respect; in whichever form you take it, go beyond it, transcend it.

Nitya dasya - you are forever, you are an eternal servant, have that feeling, "I am an eternal servant of You."

Nityakanta - I am an eternal partner of You.

Prema karyam - and that is the only thing worth doing. Even as an action, you have to do something, nothing other than just being in love.

Dasya and *kanta* - there are two major way of expressing the love. One is, "I am your obedient servant. I am the servant of the Lord. I am the servant of the Divine." But you know, in being in the Master and servant relationship, there is a little gap. There could be some hesitation, there is not that 100% closeness. So they added, *nityakanta* immediately - Your Beloved.

Both these forms of expression are not complete and they will be more complete when they are together. If someone is just your beloved, then there is always a demand on you, a demand arising in your mind. There is a chance of losing respect. Although you love them, but you demand from them, you teach them, you tell them what they should be doing. But when you are a servant - a servant never tells a Master what he should be doing. The servant and Master's relationship has a different flavour. Sometimes this, sometimes that - it gives a flavour in your life that is simply superb, that is beyond your wildest imagination. Such completeness! That of a beloved and that of a servant. A servant is not a slave you know, but he does not communicate on all levels. A beloved is one who communicates on all levels. So beloved and servant, respect and love grow together.

The love in the form of love - passion in the case of beloved, and respect in the case of Master and servant brings a completeness. And such love alone is worth having, worth expressing in life.

Bhakta ekantino mukhyah

These are the things to be done, but what is the nature of such a devotee?

God is everywhere. And what is everywhere has no value. It is commonly available everywhere. Air is available everywhere. Like air, God is everywhere. But gold is available only in gold mines, so gold has more value. In the same way, God is everywhere, but devotees are not everywhere. So devotees are more valuable than God, himself. They are more precious because this is what you cannot get. Sun is available everywhere, but diamonds are not. It is the diamond which can reflect the sun. It can shine in the sun, which can absorb the sun rays, which can reflect the sun rays totally! The one-pointedness of a devotee cannot be distracted by anybody, anything. Nothing can allure him to drop the highest, nothing can shake him, nothing can move him. *Bhakta ekantino mukhyah* - a devotee has such one-pointedness. And what do devotees do?

Kanthavarodha romancha shrubhih parasparam lapamanah pavayanti kulani prithvim cha

When devotees get together and talk, speak about the Divine, their throats choke, their hair stands up, tears roll down their eyes. *Parasparam lapamanah* - they only uplift each other. They talk about how much they miss the Divine and how much they love the Divine. This is all that they talk. *Parasparam lapamanah* - they uplift each other, they cry with each other, they talk with each other. They don't complain, there is no inquisitiveness, there is no gossiping. What is there is the earnest willingness to share the love of the Divine, the earnest desire to share the joy and the love of the Divine. They cry and cry. *Pavayanti kulani* Such devotees purify their entire family for generations of their family. Their entire system gets transformed.

See, if you keep talking negative, your system undergoes such a strain - such knots get created in your own body. And if you keep praising the Lord, praising the Divine, then your entire system undergoes a transformation. It is a scintillating experience, every cell in your body is charged up - it feels so alive, so full of love!

Pavayanti kulani prithvim cha - they purify not just their family, not just their relatives, but the whole world.

Teertha kurvanti teerthani sukarme kurvanti karmani sachchastree kurvanti shastrani

They bring holiness to the land, to the place, to the holy place. The holy place is where devotees walk, devotees sit, devotees think. That is *teertha* - that is the holy place. They make even the holy places holier. If a holy place is devoid of devotees who cry for the Divinity, it is no more holy. If a holy place is a place of fight and crime, it has lost it's vibration, it's serenity, it's holiness. How can a sacred place maintain its sacredness? It is by devotees being there, singing, praising the glory of the Divine. When such devotees walk there, the place becomes holy and they make every action holy. They make every action good action, right action. *Sachchastree kurvanti shastrani* - and they make the scriptures true, they testify the scriptures. Devotees fulfil the scriptures.

Shastrani - anyone can read a book to you, it is not a shastra. But when you hear someone reading a book and it gets into you, that is shastra. Shastra is that which directly keeps you in touch with the truth, which touches your heart. Do you see what I'm saying? Sometimes you hear something and it clicks, somewhere you feel "Yes, this is it!" That exclamation that arises in your heart, "Oh yes, I agree, I know!" - that is shastra. That is sushastra - the right scriptures, right wisdom. They bring life to wisdom. You find wisdom in all the libraries, knowledge is there everywhere in the libraries, but it doesn't integrate with life. When knowledge does not integrate with life, it does not become wisdom.

With integration of knowledge, life happens.

Sachchastree kurvanti shastrani - they are filled by him. A devotee is filled, every particle of the devotee is filled with the Divine. His heart, his mind, his breath, his body, everywhere it is only the Divine Love that is present.

Tanmayah

A devotee's glory is so much more than God Himself.

Modante pitarau nrityanti devatah, sanatha cheyam bhurbhavati

People who have crossed over, the ancestors, those who have died - they simply rejoice in the very presence of such a devotee. They simply love them, *modante pitaro nrityanti devatah, sanatha cheyam bhurbhavati* - all the angels and all the divinities - the devas, they dance. *Modante pitaro nrityanti devatah, sanatha cheyam bhurbhavati*. And this earth finds the Lord in such a devotee. The earth finds a caretaker, the earth relaxes. All the species on earth relax. There is somebody there to take care of me, who cares for me, who loves me. The earth finds a caretaker in the devotee.

All the departed souls who have left this body rejoice. They find such peace and happiness.

Nrityanthi devatah - the devas, the Divine Beings, they dance and this earth finds their Lordship.

Nasti teshu jati vidya rupa kula dhana kriyadi bhedah

Among those devotees, there is no difference of race, caste or race, or from which family they have come - high class, low class, middle class, nothing of that sort. Nor have they studied - do they have Ph.D. or are they Doctorate? The same thing said from a Doctor has a different value, as said by someone who is not a doctor. The world does not hear them. A psychologist may not know much about the mind at all, but he carries more clout than a wise person who has more knowledge about the mind. But in devotees there is no such difference.

Nasti teshu jati vidya rupa kula dhana kriyadi bhedah - religion or race, *vidya* - knowledge - how much they know, how much they do not know, or how they look, or whether they are rich or poor, or what job they do. It is immaterial. Devotees, from whichever background they come, are all the same. Because they belong to someone, they have become His.

Once the devotees have become His, become Divine, there is no distinction whatsoever - because they all belong to Him.

Yatstadiyah

That is how it is.

Om Namoh Bhagavate Vasudevaya
Om Namoh Bhagavate Vasudevaya
Om Namoh Bhagavate Vasudevaya

In order to do certain jobs, you need certain qualifications; to do certain jobs, you need certain abilities and you need strength. Strength, ability and qualification are essential for doing anything. If you want to lift 100 kilos or 100 pounds of weight, you need that much strength. Not everyone can do it. If you try and you cannot, you may sprain your back, your knees, or whatever.

So, if love is a question of ability, strength, then not everyone can love. But love transcends all ability. Whether you are a fool or a wise man, you can still be in love. Whether you are a rich person or a poor person, you can be in love. Or whether you are sick or healthy, you can be in love. Whether you are strong or weak, you can still be in love. Love transcends all these conditions. Love does not depend on your ability. It only needs a simple recognition, an acknowledgement and to acknowledge doesn't need to take a long time. Time is not a factor at all. But what can really hasten the process is the company of wise people. The company you keep can uplift your consciousness, your mind; make your heart blossom or make it shut down.

The devotees are *tanmayah* - they are filled with Him, like burning charcoal. Charcoal is black, but burning charcoal is all red. No doubt there is charcoal in it, but every particle of it is filled with fire. So you never call burning charcoal as "charcoal", you simply call it fire. Similarly, an iron rod, when it is red hot, you just call it an iron ball, it is a fireball. Though there is substance, though there are particles of iron inside, they simply get submerged in the fire, they simply get soaked in it. 'Soaked in fire' is so poetic - they are glowing with fire, every particle of the fireball. And you simply call it a ball of fire. Similarly, devotees are soaked with Divinity. *Tanmayah* - every particle of them is only saying, singing the name of the Divine. And the presence of such devotees on this planet makes the souls rejoice of all those who are dead. *Modante pitarau nrityanti devatah sanatha cheyam bhurbhavati.*

Consciousness is indestructible, like the bones in your body are indestructible. That is how they could find the bones of dinosaurs even after several million years. In the same way, if they were just left on this planet, your bones would stay forever. Like the bones, which are the grossest of your existence, and the subtlest, your consciousness, also the eternal, the mind, the consciousness which harbours the thoughts and feelings, emotions, everything, is eternal, that stays forever. And all those whose body and mind, their body and spirit have separated, that spirit still exists, the soul still exists. Those souls, those units of energy, those units of consciousness, simply rejoice in love. One ultimate question remains: how much love you have gathered in your life and have given in your life.

The flow of consciousness is towards that love, towards the Divine love, because that is the source from where it has come. In this universe everything is in a cycle. Everything goes back to its source. A deep yearning for the pinnacle of love makes this world move, move in cycles. And the angels dance, they rejoice such a Presence and the Earth finds a caretaker.

The Earth as a whole is a living organism. Don't think this Earth which harbours so many varieties of life is dead, is just an object. No, it is conscious, it has life. Only life can bring up life. If this planet is dead, if there is no feeling, no consciousness in the Earth as a whole, how can it harbour so many species which has consciousness? Do you see what I am saying?

Like your body - do you consider it only as matter? Is your hand only matter? No doubt it is matter, but there is consciousness in it. Like your physical body, though matter, harbours life, this universe, this world, this Earth harbours a Big Mind, the Consciousness; it has its own life. The next sutra says :

Vado navalambyah

Don't depend on logic. You cannot catch love through logic. Logic cuts, logic analyzes, it tears things apart. But love is just the opposite - it brings everything together. Love is a process of uniting; logic is a method to analyze, to separate. *Vado navalambyah* - arguments are not to be depended upon. The moment you start arguing, you simply indicate that you are not in agreement, isn't that so? You know, when you argue, you think the other is not getting you right. That is when you try to convince them and argue, explaining to them. To clear misunderstandings you sometimes start arguing or explaining which creates more confusion, more misunderstanding. How many of you have had this experience?

If you just keep quiet, everything would have cleared by itself. But we argue and make our position correct. We want to convince someone of our correctness and we fail miserably. Even if you convince the other persons of your correctness, they are really not convinced. Because this argument you had has already created a distance, has already put a sourness in the milk.

Bahulyavakashavad aniya tatvacha

Because logic has many possibilities. You can use the same logic to prove something or to disprove something - ask lawyers! Any point can be taken to prove something or to disprove the same thing. So *bahulyavakashavad* - there are so many possibilities in logic. I have said earlier there are three types of logic: One is Tarka which means pure logic. And then Kutarka, wrong logic. And Vitarka is qualified logic.

I will give you an example. If a door is half-open, that means it is half-shut - that is logic.

Wrong logic : if the door is half-open, we agree it is half-closed. So if it is fully open, then it must be fully closed! This is called kutarka, wrong logic. The flower is on the table and the table is on the floor, so the flower is on the floor. This is wrong logic. Through this wrong logic, or Kutarka, only ignorance increases.

And Vitarka is such a logic, such an inference, it simply amazes you. "Who am I? What is this all about? What is Life? Who are You? Who am I?" This is called vitarka. This understanding that you are going through now, this moment, is also logic, but it is vitarka, qualified logic.

So do not depend on arguments. Argument indicates lack of unity from the level of the heart. Often when you are studying under a teacher, under a Master, especially in the Zen tradition, they would never allow you to argue. If it is said, "It is sunny outside," maybe even in the middle of the night, You would have to say, "Yes, I'm sweating!"

Truth is beyond arguments, beyond discussions. Arguments are in vain. It is all just words, trying to convince someone that you are right. But in the field of love, that does not work. That is why so many love affairs break, because they start depending on some logic, some arguments. Arguments to convince that they love the other person much more! "No, I really love you, because, see, I did this, I did this, I did this, took you to this place, I took you…. You think I don't care for you?" Arguments and arguments and arguments…

Vado navalambya - there are so many possibilities in logic, in arguments, do not sit and argue. If someone is negative or accusing you, give them a smile. They are venting it all out. This is the first procedure to adopt. "Oh is it so? I acknowledge your feelings, I honour your feelings." And reflect within yourself what is that you feel - is there any truth to what the other person has told you? If there is truth, thank them. If there is no truth in it, be compassionate to them, give them more wisdom. Help them to uplift their own state of mind. There is no better service than helping someone to uplift their state of mind, because that will make them stand on their feet, that will make them come out of their own misery. Otherwise you give people everything else but if you do not tell them or teach them how to come out of their own misery, they will still be in misery. Each person will have to take the responsibility for their miserable attitudes, miserable conditions.

Vado navalambyah - don't depend on arguments because there are so many possibilities. Someone says, "You have to go west in order to go to Los Angeles." Another person says, "No no, you can go through east also." Tell them, "Yes, I agree, it is a longer route, but you can go through east also." There are so many possibilities.

Bhakti shastrani mananiyani tadudbodhaka karmani karaneyani

The scriptures which talk about love will have to be learned and heard, understood and digested. And the actions that they say there will have to be followed. Here Narada says this, because you can say that this also is a logic. 'If you say you don't have to apply logic, that is also logic! Say, yes, yes, of course, I say no need of studying books and scriptures and this and that, but still you need something, so learn these sutras, learn this knowledge. When you are listening to it, just don't think you have listened to it once, and finished! These 84 sutras that he has said here, listen to them again and again, because every time you hear it, every time you practice it, it takes you deeper, it uplifts you to another level.

Knowledge is structured in consciousness. And as you grow, your consciousness expands, the knowledge also changes. *Tadudbodhak karmani karaneyani* - and you need to do all the service activity and the actions that have been prescribed in your path, that have been asked of you to do. If you have to do pranayama, continue doing pranayama. Don't think, "Oh, there is no qualification needed in order to be in love. I don't need to do anything. Guruji has said no need to. Why should I sit and meditate at all?" No, do it, because it will take you deeper.

Sukha dukha ichcha labhadityakte kaale prateekshamane kshanardhamapi vyartham na neyam

There is no need to get caught up in pleasure and pain, in desires. "I want this, I want that," these desires, pain, pleasure, this tendency of wanting to know, what will I gain - no need to get caught up.

Buddha was asked, "What did you gain in your Enlightenment?" He said, "Nothing. But I lost a lot of things." "What do you gain by meditation?" He said, "No, I lost a lot of things." The goal is right where you are! What you want to gain is already there! Just stop, relax.

Once a devotee was given a boon. A devotee was praying and God was pleased with his prayers and said, "Okay what is that you want?" He said, "God, I want plenty of land." God said, "Okay, do

107

one thing. As far as you can run, that much land is all yours. How far can you run? Go that far - upto that point all the land belongs to you. You can own it, you can take all the riches from the land, the goldmine and whatever is present, it is all yours."

So he ran and ran and ran and ran. But wherever he would stop, he would say, "Oh, I see more mountains there, maybe I can go up to that mountain." So he would run up to that. When he went there, he found other landscape even more beautiful. So, the farther he went, the farther he found it much more beautiful. Then he found the sea. He said, "This sea is so beautiful! I must have this sea! Because this has oil, this has pearls, fishes, this has everything! How can I refuse the sea! I need the sea also." So he swam across and he went round and round and round and... non-stop.

Finally he dropped dead in one place! Greed made him run and run and run and finally, when he came back, he just dropped dead. How much land he had wanted, just that he occupied! 6 feet 2 inches! No more. For this much land he ran all over the world, the whole time trying to possess it!

There is a similar story about Alexander the Great. He conquered most of Middle East and Europe and then when he came to India, someone presented him a golden bread on a plate. He was so hungry. He came to a village and they gave him golden bread. In those days India was very, very rich. That is how Columbus tried to find India and landed up in America. This is before Columbus, much earlier. So when he was presented with golden bread, he said, "No, no, I want real bread!"

Said one simple peasant there, "Oh, I thought you were an emperor, you will only eat gold! Do you want wheat bread?"

He said, "Yes!"

"Don't you get this wheat bread from where you are, where you were? Do you have to conquer all these places to eat the same wheat bread? I also eat the same wheat bread and you also eat the wheat bread! And for that you have to kill so many hundreds and thousands of people all over the world, conquering everywhere...!"

Someone had told Alexander the Great that when you go to India, you will find sadhus there, saints. Just catch hold of one of them and bring them along. They have a lot of wisdom, a lot of knowledge. There is a story that he tried to take back one to Greece.

But when he died, he told his minister, " Keep my hands open, both palms open. Let the whole world know Alexander conquered the world, but he went with empty hands, nothing in his hands." He died without reaching his land - only his body came back. The greed is what keeps one going and going - one more, one more, one more.

How much more can you have? More happiness. This more and more is on which the mind gallops. It is aaid lover is in the present, a devotee is in the moment. *Now* and *here*. Says, "I am satisfied." And that is why Jesus said, "Those who have shall be given more. Those who do not, whatever little they have, that will also be taken away." That contentment that you have uplifts you, elevates you.

Once a retired Chief Justice of Supreme Court of India came to me and said, "Guruji, I want your blessings." I said, "What for?" (Laughter) Sometimes I ask, "Blessings for what? No blank cheque issued - purpose to be indicated! (Laughter)
He said, "Guruji, I have just one more desire. I have everything, just one more thing I desire. I want to be in the International Court of Justice. I want to reach the Hague."
I looked at him and said, "Look, you have attained the highest position in this country. And if you are not satisfied, if you are frustrated, think about all those lower court lawyers and judges working there, how frustrated they would be?"
"Yes, I understand, but just this one desire, please give a blessing for it. It is not for me, it is for the benefit of the whole world! I want

to be in a position so that I can serve you better!"

No. This is all fooling yourself. The greed - *labhadi*, how much you can see for pleasure. Or misery - don't get stuck up if you are miserable. Open your eyes and look at all those who are much more miserable than you. You will find your misery is nothing, it is too small. If you are miserable, you have not opened your eyes and seen around. If you see around, you will see you are not miserable.

Kaale prateekshamaane - have patience. "Oh this is all wonderful, but I don't feel that love. I hear, it's all nice, I sing, I dance, but I don't feel those things. When will I feel them?" Don't worry. Just have patience.

Someone said, "Oh, twenty years I am meditating. I have been on so many advanced programmes, meditated so long, I have sung, I have done this japa, I have done that practice, nothing is happening." Just have patience, just have patience. If nothing has been happening, you would not continue anything! Why did you do twenty years of meditation if nothing has happened? Changes are happening. Maybe they are slow, maybe you are unable to notice them. Never mind. Have patience. Don't waste even a second. You know, we waste a lot of time in trivial things, such unimportant things. Our mind, our heart, our time is all wasted in such things. Be enthusiastic. Keep the spirit up. We have come to this planet with tears in our eyes, kicking and crying we came here - we should not exit the same way, kicking and crying! Make a difference. At least when you leave this planet, go with a big smile, with such celebration.

Ahimsa, satya, shaucha, daya, aastikyadi, charitrayani paripalniyani

What do the scriptures say? What is that you have to do in order to be in such Divine love, in order to be a devotee? What is that you have to do in order to be a devotee?

It says the first principle is non-violence. A devotee cannot afford to be violent. The owner of this universe is with you, what is that you need to be afraid of? Violence is a sign of weakness. Violence indicates that you are fearful, you have no support, you have no strength. When you have the greatest support with you, when you own the greatest support of this universe, where is the fear? How can you be afraid of anything? People who are violent are often scared. They have fear fermenting in them. They are afraid of losing something, so they become violent.

Ahimsa - non-violence is the first principle.

Satya - truth, to be with what is.

Shaucha means cleanliness, inner and outer cleanliness, yes? The mind becoming clean, free. That is what meditation does to you. When you go deep in mediation, what happens? When you do Sudarshan Kriya or pranayama, what happens to you? All that negativity just leaves you, drops out of the system... inner and outer cleanliness.

Daya - compassion and *Faith* in a Divine existence.

All these values need to be absorbed. You need to observe these laws. Though lovers have no rules - there is no rule that you have to express your love only like this, say only this at such a time. Emotions and feelings are spontaneous and their expression is also spontaneous. There cannot be a military rule in expressing your love. It is not a regiment, like a parade where you put your left foot out, or right foot, and you walk like you are in a parade. That is discipline, not a spontaneous expression of love. Discipline and spontaneity are completely opposite, yet they complement each other. This is the paradox here. On one side, Narada is talking about love which transcends all disciplines. Love means chaos - and utter chaos! Divine love is utter chaos!

But yet, he says, certain discipline you need to follow so that there is chaos in discipline and discipline in chaos. They complement somewhere on some deep level. Lovers do not like any discipline. Any discipline will suffocate them, they want freedom. That is why they are paradoxical.

Devotion is a path of freedom. The path of love is that of freedom. You have absolute freedom to express your love, but yet, he says, you need to have certain disciplines. What are the disciplines? *Ahimsa*, non-violence. So that your freedom does not infringe on someone else's freedom, your love does not suffocate someone else and become violence for them. *Satya*-truth, *Shaucha*-purity, *Daya*-compassion and *faith* in the Divine existence will all have to be followed.

Worship is Inevitable

Sarvada sarvabhavena nishchinteh Bhagavaneva bhajaniyah

Sa keertamanah sheeghramevavirbhava atyanubhavayati cha bhaktan

Trisatyasya bhaktireva gareeyasi, bhaktireva gareeyasi

Gunmahatmyasakti roopasakti poojasakti smaranasakti dasyasakti sakhyasakti, vatsalyasakti Kantasakti atmanivedanasakti tanmayatasakti

Pramavirahasakti roopa ekadha api ekadashadha bhavati

Om Namoh Bhagavate Vasudevaya
Om Namoh Bhagavate Vasudevaya
Om Namoh Bhagavate Vasudevaya

Love and discipline are two extreme aspects of reality. When there is love, you don't need to concentrate on the work you do. Discipline, or concentration, is essential when there is no love. When there is love, the mind becomes still, the mind stays there. There is no need to concentrate or to focus. Someone who loves astronomy doesn't need to discipline himself in order to learn astronomy - not twenty-four hours at least. And when a physicist is in love with his subject, he does not need to concentrate - he loves what he does.

So there are no rules, there are no disciplines applicable to love. Yet there are certain things that need to be followed in order to preserve the delicate state of existence deep within you. What are these rules? Narada says that to maintain this state, non-violence is to be practiced. Because they do not match with love. Divine love is so delicate. Someone who is very subtle or delicate cannot be aggressive - they are two extremes. Aggression can only happen with insensitivity, with inertia. Love makes you utterly sensitive. To be violent you need a certain amount of 'thick' skin, but love makes you so delicate from the depth. Love distorts and becomes hatred, but love can never disappear. To maintain the Divine love you need to follow certain principles which are essential, that is non-violence, truth, purity, compassion and faith in the Divine.

113

Sarvada sarvabhavena nishchinteh Bhagavaneva bhajaniyah

But life is not all that smooth all the time, it is not so delicate all the time. So, what to do? Sometimes you get upset, sometimes you get irritated; you cannot maintain a single mood throughout life. Moods are like clouds, they are not stationary, same with feelings. In pooja you offer flowers, when someone comes to you, you offer them flowers. You know what is the significance of flowers? Flowers signify feelings. If you go to the Orient or even to Hawaai, you are given a wreath, a flower garland - an expression of feelings. Our feelings are like flowers - they are there, they blossom, they stay for sometime and then they die out. Feelings are not paper flowers which stay for ever. They are real flowers - they come up, they blossom and they die out - and new flowers blossom. Every day, new feelings come. You can never have stale love, yesterday's love - this moment it is fresh, new, it blossoms.

That is why we never get bored in love. *Sarvada sarvabhavena* - all the time, in all modes, always, in all moods of the mind, in all feelings, consciousness. *Nishchinteh Bhagavaneva bhajaniyah* - without worrying, dwell only on the Divine. One who worries does not know Divinity. It is as simple as that.

See, when you worry, you are caught up in the head; at some place, when the worry breaks, some feelings arise. Are you getting what I am saying? Children don't worry, but they are emotional. They get angry so totally - every cell in the body vibrates with anger. They scream, the anger emits from every pore of their body. When they are happy, they laugh from their entire Being. Worry is getting stuck up there in the head. It is better to cry, laugh and enliven the feeling within you instead of worrying - worry makes you so inert, heavy, dull. It is like a stone sitting on the head. Your brain freezes in

114

worry, but feelings warm your heart, clothe your body. You have no control over feelings, absolutely no control over your feelings. The Rishi here does not say that you should control your feelings, but you can have a say over your worries because worry is self-generated. Worry is of limited understanding. Worry comes up only when you understand very little, when your perception is limited, when you don't know the big picture, then your mind goes on and gallops on the horse of thoughts. Feelings you have no control over and many types of feelings come.

All the time, the Rishi says, *Sarvada sarvabhavena* - all the time, in all moods, in all feelings; *nishchinteh Bhagavaneva bhajaniyah* - without worrying adore the Divinity, wherever you see, see the Divinity there. A guest comes to your home, treat them as Divine. Treat children as Divine, treat your parents as Divine. See the Divinity everywhere. Someone is upset with you - treat that also as Divine. Today this particular Divine is upset with me! (Laughter) If you want to get upset, get upset. In the previous sutra Narada has said, "If you want to be angry, be angry at the Divine. Don't be angry at small things. It is not worth it." No one else is worth investing so much of your energy. You have to invest so much of your energy in anger. Be like a child - flow with the emotions, if it needs to be; it is better than sitting and being caught up in this small mind that worries. The worry is all about, "What about me?" When you own the Lord of this creation, where is, "What about me?" It has no meaning.

Sa keertimanah sheeghramevavirbhava atyanubhavayati cha bhaktan

And when you really sing with all your heart, when you really want the Divinity, he comes to you as an experience. Sing - *keertimanah*, means like a child crying. A child cries from its whole being. He puts body, breath, soul - everything. Similarly, when you

115

are singing from your heart, when you long for the Divine, that Divinity comes quickly - *sheeghrameva* - it is not that you call and he comes after ten years . You call the Divine and it is the sincerity in your calling, "Knock and it shall be opened, ask and it shall be given." That is exactly it, it is so obvious.

Trisatyasya bhaktireva gareeyasi, bhaktireva gareeyasi

There are three truths, three paths - the path of knowledge, the path of action and the path of love. You can attain something through these three ways - through knowledge, action and love.

Deep analysis, sharp attention and flawless perception take you to the knowledge which is truth, which is ultimate.

Precise action and 100% dedicated swift and compassion will take you to the same reality, same goal.

And blemishless love, unconditional and Universal, takes you to the same goal.

So, of these three paths of knowledge, action and devotion, the path of love, of devotion is supreme. Because for knowledge you need some abilities, to go on the path of action you need strength, but to love you need nothing.

To gain knowledge, you need patience, perseverence and clear perception. To engage yourself in action, you need strength and right observation and correction - action always needs correction. Not every step in the action will be the same, so it needs the observation and the ability to correct the next step. But the path of love needs nothing. It needs just one thing and that is the recognition that the Divines loves you so dearly. You cannot be in Divine love if you do not know the Divine loves you so dearly. First God tells you, "I love you so much, that is why I have created this beautiful world for you," and just a recognition of the unconditional love of the Divine is good enough for you to be on the path of love. And this recognition, you can make it now, in this moment, or after several lifetimes - it is up to you! Just that faith, unquestioning faith that the Divine loves you so dearly, "Anything in the world may change, but not the love of the Divine for me." This strong conviction, faith in the Divine love is essential to walk the path of love - it is the only qualification.

If you doubt the love of the Divine for you, then you will stumble, you may not be able to walk the path of love. Never ever doubt the love of the Divine, however seemingly it may appear to be contrary to you. It may appear that the Divine does not love, but don't even take notice of it.

Bhaktireva gareeyasi - of the three truths, love alone is supreme. And there are eleven different types of love. Though Divine love is only one, there are eleven different types of love.

Gunmahatmyasakti roopasakti poojasakti
Smaranasakti dasyasakti sakhyasakti vatsalyasakti
Kantasakti atmanivedanasakti tanmayatasakti
Paramavirhasakti rupa ekadha api ekadashadha bhavati

Though it is only one, there are eleven flavours to it. You know, you go to Hagen Daas, though it is the same basic icecream, you have so many flavours - pistachio, vanilla, and what ever. The spirit loves diversity. Spirit is not so dry and monotonous. Divinity loves diversity. Look at the creation - are there one type of fruit in the whole creation? Nature could have created just one type of vegetable - pumpkins, only pumpkins. Year long, pumpkins all over the world, no other vegetable, or maybe only carrots. Suppose the creation had only apples and you had no idea about any other fruit at all? Can you imagine the world like this? It would be so boring. The nature loves diversity, the spirit loves variety - it loves different manifestations. God loves variety. And do you think that the Divinity which loves variety does not love the variety in love also?

The ancient Rishi sages, they knew this - the innermost secrets, they mysteries of the Universe - they saw that this Divinity has so many names, so many forms, manifest in so many ways. God is one, yet, he has many attributes, many forms and many names. Like you are a human being, right? Yet you are a father to somebody and you are brother to somebody else. And a husband, too. How can you be a father and son at the same time? Don't you have many facets to your life? Don't you have many roles in your life? Can your brother be also a son or a father? A woman is not just a wife. She is also a sister, a mother, she is also a daughter. Similarly if you are a doctor and working somewhere, when you are sick, you are a patient. Doctors can also be patients, no? You are a lawyer but you can be a client somewhere else, when it comes to your income tax. (Laughter) So you have many roles in your life to play and that is what the Rishis have said - it is true there is one Divinity, but He has many different roles. He creates sometimes and He destroys some other time and He has another role of maintaining and they call by different names.

That impulse of intelligence which is responsible for creation is different from the impulse of creation that brings the fall and destroys. Those impulses which are there in Spring are different from those which are there in the Fall. And they gave different names - *Brahma*. The role of the Divine as Brahma is to create. When a CEO is driving a car, he is a driver at that time. When he goes to his table, he is a CEO but when he is at home playing with the kids, he is a father. The same Divinity in some place is Brahma, in some place is Vishnu - when maintaining and then in some place is Shiva - transforming, bringing new things; he is effecting a change to an existing system, that is Shiva. They call it by these different names, by the roles of that intelligence.

Similarly Love also assumes eleven flavours.

The first he says is *Gunmahatmyasakti* - when you are in love with somebody, you dwell on their qualities, you adore their qualities *Gunmahatmyasakti* - such great qualities so and so has, that person is so beautiful.Admiring the qualities, the wisdom - *gunmahatmyasakti*. Admiring this whole creation in all its flavours, that is *gunmahatmyasakti* - the love for the glory and the qualities that the Divine exhibits.

Rupasakti - adoring the form. So many forms this universe has, and every form indicates the one Divinity. Adoring the Divine in the forms. This *asakti* word doesn't really have a parallel in English - adoring, adoring the forms, the varieties in creation, *roopasakati* - the form of the Divine. Love cannot be experienced without the form to begin with. You can love a baby, but you cannot love the empty space next to the baby. You can love a dog, but you cannot love the empty space next to the dog. Though spirit is like space, spirit is not just the body. You can love a person, but how can you express your love to something which you don't know, an empty space? Form has become an inevitable thing, although the Divine is formless. In Islam, Mohammad removed all the forms, he said, "God is Formless," which is the reality. God is formless. But how do you adore God which is formless? (Later some letters occupied the place of figures.) Certain people cannot be without forms. It takes them a little while to transcend the form. So, finally Mohammad had to lower the Kaba stone and that Kaba stone fulfilled the need for the form for the people. Although stones or other idols are not worshipped, but the Kaba stone is a symbol of a form, it stands as a symbol; the cresecent moon and the star is a symbol of a form. A form had to be brought in because there was a need for the people. How do they identify something with something? The Cross is a form. You know, when people are in love, or in devotion, they make a cross on themselves, feel that cross - a form you are attached to. Or *Om...* Hindus take Om as a form, the Shivaling as a form. The Parsis worship fire as the form. Some symbol comes up and this is also a love - interested in the form.

Poojasakti - love the form and then adore the form - worship. Pooja means that which is born out of fullness. *Poo* means fullness, *ja* means born out of fullness. In love, when you feel so full, you want to act, do something and that act which is born out of love is called Pooja. *Poojasakti* - in pooja you use all the five elements, all that nature has done to you, you replicate it, you do it back again. What did the nature do to you? It has given you grains, the nature has given you grains ... you offer the grains. The nature has given you flowers, you offer the flowers. Nature has given you fruits, so you offer the fruits back. Nature takes the sun and moon around you and you also light the camphor on a small wick or candle and you also move them around. That is called *aarti* - the ultimate ecstacy. *Aarti* means the ultimate ecstacy, because nature is doing *aarti* to you every day - taking the sun and moon around you. Remembering that let this fire of life always move around the Divine. Life is like fire, goes up, you know a lit fire or a glow, if you turn it upside down, then also it just moves up. Let the enthusiasm, that joy in life, always move upward. This feeling you take - *pooja sakti*.

Smarnasakti - constant rememberance of the divine. It is almost like a worry. You know, when you are worried, as soon as you wake up in the morning, the same worry comes to the head. And before going to bed, the same worry comes. While you are eating, same worry comes. When you're drinking tea, same worry comes. So, dwelling in the same memory of the Divine is another type of love - *smarnasakti*.

Dasyasakti - wanting to be the servant of God. the Jewish

Tradition has glorified this, being the servant of God. That aspect of love is emphasised in Jewish Tradition - "I am just a servant of God, I am nothing other than a simple servant of God." *Dasya sakti* - to be a devoted servant.

Sakhayasakti - companionship. He is my companion. I am his companion. There are two different things. One is *dasyasakti* - "I am just a servant of God" and then, "I am his companion. He is my only companion." The saints of the Bhakti movement in India all adored God as the beloved, their companion. The Gopis took God as their beloved, their companion. In the Muslim Tradition, some Sufi saints also consider God as their beloved. *Sakhya sakti* - taking God as one's beloved.

Vatsalyasakti - considering God as one's child. In Brindavan in India, people consider Krishna as their own child - *Bal*. When a child is born in the house, they say, "Oh, Krishna has come." *Infant Jesus* worship is also prevalent in some parts of the world. There is a certain charm, a certain motherly or fatherly feeling towards the Divine. 'Parenting the Divine' is another form of Divine love.

Kantasakti - is one's own partner. God as the centre of attraction of all sorts in life. "My only goal and my only centre of attraction is Divinity." This feeling that comes up in you, that God is only centre of atraction, is *Kantasakti*. You adore the Divine as your beloved, as your partner, as a part of you - *Kantasakti*.

Atmanivedanasakti - every moment this entire body, mind - physical, mental, emotional, my entire life is all yours. I offer, I surrender everything, every moment, including the time, this moment is yours. If this moment is pleasant, it is yours. If it is unpleasant, it is yours. Who cares, it is all yours. *Atmanivedanasakti* - offering of the entire self, your total self, total letting go, that is *atmanivedanasakti* - another flavour of love.

Tanmayatasakti means being immersed in knowing that he is already in you and every part is immersed in him, soaked in the Divinity. *Tanmayata* is also a deep meditation, a state of deep meditation, a state in which you forget everything else, nothing exists, nothing whatsoever exists, just me and me alone. *Tanmayatasakti* - forgetful of everything else, including your own body, that is *tanmayata*. Those that forget everything are really blissful. A lady once said, "Guruji, I keep forgetting everything." I said, "Wonderful, don't worry about it. The whole essence is to forget everything. Why do you have to remember anything? Just be happy." An ability to forget everything - we often forget all the nice things, the good things, and remember only those unwanted, horrible things that stick to the mind. That shift is essential. If you want to forget, forget everything - *tanmayatasakti*.

Paramvirahasakti means longing, excruciatating longing. There is a joy in longing. Love blossoms only in longing. If there is no longing, I tell you there is no love also. Love and longing go hand in hand, so when longing arises in you, don't kill it. Though it is excrucitating, don't try to run away from it. Nurture the longing. Nurturing the longing deepens the love. Often, when longing comes, people run away from it and then the love turns into hatred and anger. Longing brings a certain amount of misery - you don't like anything, you don't want to eat, you don't want to see television, you don't want to go anywhere, nothing is appealing to you, that is the name of longing. These are the characteristics of longing. Longing means what? Nothing whatsoever can charm you, can interest you, can draw your attention, nor are you at peace.

A totally disturbed state of mind is longing! And you need to enjoy the totally disturbed state also. You know, there is a threshold, and you have to cross the threshold to bear that longing, otherwise that longing creates blame. This happens among lovers. They cannot handle their longing, so they keep blaming each other for their misery. And they say, "Look how much I love you, look what you do - you make me wait for an hour, is this fair to me? What else is more important for you? Maybe your mind is somewhere else? Maybe you don't love me? Maybe we made a mistake." All this paraphernalia crops up. You create a web around you and you get sucked into it. It is your own web that you create.

Longing is excruciating and that threshold of longing has to be crossed and you find that there is such sweetness in longing. This is the love between Radha and Krishna - there was so much longing between them and so much love. There is a nice story about Radha and Krishna. Radha and Krishna were going for a walk in the evening in the forest and Krishna said, "Look Radha, these flowers are so beautiful, these trees are so beautiful." And Radha said, "Yes, they are reflecting your beauty, my dear Lord." Krishna says, "They are beautiful just because you are looking at them. If you were not to look, they wouldn't look so beautiful. It is the reflection of your sight that is shining and making them so beautiful." It was sweet talk. You know, usually when lovers talk, they don't make much sense. A scientist is completely baffled by lovers' talk. And then they said, "Let's play something." Then Radha said, "Okay, I'll hide and you search me." They were small you know. Krishna was about 14 years old and Radha was older than Krishna by two or three years.

So, Radha hid herself in the forest somewhere and Krishna went around looking for her. He searched her here, there, everywhere and within a few minutes, maybe 20-30 minutes, he got restless because he could not find her. And the longing became more and more and he became miserable. Then he just sat in one place, absolutely miserable because he couldn't find Radha. They both had a common friend whose name was Lalita. Lalita came and asked, "Oh my dear Krishna, what are you doing? Why are you so miserable?" He said, "You know, I can't find Radha. Now my hands are shivering, my legs are shivering, I can't take a step anymore. I can't move an inch from here, so you have to help me."

And she says, "Okay, don't worry, I will find Radha. I know how to get her." So Lalita goes searching and she finds Radha in some place hiding. She says, "You know, Krishna is so upset and so miserable that he couldn't find you." Just hearing the words that Krishna is miserable, Radha says, "See, I am paralysed now. I can't move a step, my hands, everything is frozen. I was the cause for his misery. I cannot take it that I became the cause for the misery of my Lord. You only do something." So she collapsed there, fainted. Now Lalita got even more upset. She didn't know what to do, how to bring them together. Then Lalita ran back to Krishna to give him the message that she has found Radha. By that time, Krishna was sitting there and meditating, and when she reached there to give the news, Krishna opened his eyes and showed that Radha is just next to him, by his side. What does that mean? When your mind which is running, when it goes inside, when it goes to the source, right there you find the beloved. Lalita, the common friend, means descrimination.

You know when ancient people wrote stories, they didn't make just some story, they put some symbolism in it. They put some wisdom in it so that the story became an immortal story. When love and longing were there and they both were miserable, discrimination or wisdom was essential. Wisdom came and recognised that the beloved is right there. When the mind becomes quiet and one goes inward, there is no distance. Lalita means wisdom, united. So they were always united, they were never separated, Radha and Krishna.

Women were given prime place in the Vedic traditions. That is why you always say womens' name first and then mens' name, Radha and then Krishna, Laxmi and Narayan, Gauri and Shankar. Women were given foremost importance. And the three important porfolios were all given to women - finance, defence and education! All the important portfolios were given to women in the cosmic field, in the Deva's field - the field of angels. Women control the wealth of the Universe, women control the knowledge and the defence.

Paramavirahasakti - an intense longing, nurturing and enjoying the longing. A devotee once said, "Guruji, please don't come to our city." I thought it is a very strange request as usually everyone keeps requesting me to visit their city. "The longing is so excruciating, it is so enjoyable, I don't want this longing to go away. Oh please don't come to the city." *Pramavirahasakti.*

Rupa ekadhapi ekadashadha bhavati - though it is one, it has all these eleven flavours. And there are so many examples and stories about each, depiciting each one of these types of love and devotion. There are so many stories of so many kings and so many people who have nourished these flavours of life. *Ekadha api* - though it is one, it finds its expression in eleven flavours.

Next, Narada says :

Iti evam vadanti janjalpa anirbhayah ekmatah
Kumar Vyasa Shuka Shandilyah Gargah Vishnu
Kaundinya Sheshudhava Arun Bali
Hanumad Vibhishan dayo bhaktya charyah

Narada says all those Gurus or Acharyas who have expounded on devotion so say and he named the thirteen great saints, great Masters who have expounded, who have *lived* the love - not just written some treatise. No - life has been that way. Each of their story is so inspiring - 13 Acharyas. These Masters did not care for what people would think about them - they were fearless about the comments of people. *Janjalpa anirbhayah* - they are not bothered about what people will think or comment about them. They have

125

become perfect in the path of devotion.

Society wants you to be reasonable, love is beyond reason. Society binds you with logic and rules, love is beyond logic and rules. Society can accept a philosopher, but it finds it difficult to accept somebody crazy - singing and dancing, having their own world.

A devotee has his own world because his world is nothing but God. Nobody exists except God. When only God exists, He does not react to anything anybody says. Nobody can push his buttons - that is the state of a devotee. His devotion is foremost. That is all what his life is. Maybe people will comment - so what? How does it matter to him? There is a flow which has no resistance from a devotee, he is fearless. Fear comes when you have a defence in you. Defence create fear, but we understand it completely the other way around. The very fact of your defence indicates fear - *janjalpa anirbhayah.*

And lovers have never fought - they always say the same thing, all lovers are of the same opinion. Anyone who will taste sugar will say the same thing - one will not say sugar is bitter, another will not say sugar is salty. That is how it is! Although their words may be different, their flavours of devotion may be different, but they all agree in one thing - that is Divine love, *ekmatah*!

Sant Kumara was the Guru of Narada, and then Vyasa, then Shukadeva, Shandilyah, Gargah, then Vishnu, Kaundinya, Sheshudhava, Bali, Hanumad, Vibhishan - the thirteen teachers, Masters who lived love in its totality, in its infinity...no, it is wrong to use the word totality - knowledge can be total, love cannot be.

Last sutra :

Yah idam Narada proktam Shivanushasanam
vishwasiti shradhate sa bhaktiman bhavate

126

sah preshtham labhate, sah preshtham labhate
Om tat sat

These are the aphorisms of love of Narada, and whoever believes in them, trusts in them, has *shradha* in them, will definitely attain the Divine love.

You have to trust something - you have to trust that you exist. You have to trust in the world. You will have to trust the earth that you walk on - without trust, nothing can happen in society, in life, in the world. Even if you try to mistrust totally, you cannot - trust dawns magically. The fullness of trust is Divine, is God.

You know, you trust what you have seen and what you feel - this is world. Trust in what you just hear (you have not seen) - that is God. What you see is not true, but what you hear is true. You see the sun setting but you have heard the sun does not set, isn't it? You see the world so permanent, non-changing, but you have heard from science that every atom is changing all the time.

Yah idam Narada proktam - these aphorisms which have been said by Narada a very auspicious.

Shivanushasanam - it is these sutras, this knowledge that can lift you up, that can hold you back from following, that can save you from misery and put you right on to yourself.

Shivanushasanam vishwasiti shradhate sa bhaktiman bhavate - he will definitely attain the Divine love, he will be full of devotion - *sah preshtham labhate, sah preshtham labhate*. He will realise the most beloved Divine, he will attain the highest goal in life.

This is a promise that Narada makes in the end. Usually people make a promise in the beginning, but Narada gives you the promise at the end. Even after hearing all this, if a doubt arises in your mind, he says, "Okay, you may doubt me, but all these other Acharyas have also said the same thing."

You shop in many places, but everybody will tell you to dig deep. Wherever you dig, you will have to dig deep - there is no use digging 2 feet in 10 places...

Have faith, go deep - you will definitely attain.

Sah preshtham labhate, sah preshtham labhate
You will have it, soon you will have it - I promise you.

The International Art of Living Foundation

The Art of Living Foundation (www.artofliving.org) is devoted to making life a celebration. A non-profit educational organization run by volunteers, it offers programmes for self-development and spiritual growth that allow even the busiest of people to take maximum advantage of *Sri Sri's* multidimensional teachings. The Foundation is recognized as an official Non-Governmental Organization (NGO) of the United Nations, developing and sponsoring service projects worldwide, including programmes for people living with HIV and cancer, rehabilitative training for prisoners and vocational training for rural and under-privileged people.

The "Dollar-a-Day"programme (www.careforchildren.org) provides children with food, clothing and education.

Founded in 1981, and accredited as a charitable nonprofit institution, **Ved Vignan Mahavidyapeeth** (Institute of Vedic Science) provides many essential educational and medical services. The only source of free education in the rural area surrounding Bangalore, India, this top-rated Institute serves almost a thousand boys and girls from 22 villages. Books, uniforms, meals, medical check-ups, pick-up and drop-off at their homes are all provided at no charge to each child through funding from supporting individuals and groups.

The internationally acclaimeded **5-H Programme** (www.5H.org) is a joint effort of *Vyakti Vikas Kendra* in India and the *International Association for Human Values* (www.IAHV.org). It offers social and community development projects with a focus on Health, Hygiene, Homes, Harmony in diversity and Human values. This unique and comprehensive approach involves training youths to become community leaders. Thousands of people have benefited through training programmes, cleaning drives, health camps, construction of bore-wells, toilet blocks and septic systems, while more than 500 homes have been provided in villages of India, alone.

The Art of Living Workshop

The Art of Living workshop is the cornerstone of Sri Sri's wisdom. The 16–18-hour programme is usually offered over six days and has uplifted the lives of more than one million people worldwide. Breath contains the secret of life and is a link to vital life energy, or prana. Low prana causes depression, lethargy, dullness and poor enthusiasm. A mind and body charged with prana is alert, energetic and happy. Specific breathing techniques taught on the course revitalize and invigorate both physical and emotional well-being. Among these techniques is a powerful process called Sudarshan Kriya, which fully oxygenates the cells, recharging them with new energy and life, washing away negative emotions stored as toxins in the body. Tension, anger, anxiety, depression and lethargy are released and forgotten. The mind is left calm and centred, with a clearer vision of the world, relationships and and our own self. The course also includes processes and deep insights into the nature of life and happiness.

For further deatils, contact your nearest Centre - listed on page 137.

Advanced Courses are specially designed for those who have completed the Art of Living Course. These retreats, spent partially in silence, provide a profound opportunity to explore the depths of our own inner silence through deep meditation, service and enjoyable processes. Each evening ends with a celebration of singing, dancing and astounding wisdom. One leaves feeling renewed emotionally and elevated spiritually, with a dynamism for greater success in one's activities. Some Advanced Courses are offered in Sri Sri's presence, which is the experience of a lifetime.

Sahaj Samadhi Meditation is another gift from *Sri Sri*. Not one of us lacks spiritual depth. The peace and happiness we seek in the world is already within us, but masked by stress and strain. Sahaj

Samadhi Meditation provides a rest much deeper than sleep, releasing deep-rooted stresses and energizing our nervous systems. Stress drops off, the chattering mind becomes serene and creative, aging slows and one rediscovers the unshakable contentment of one's inner Self. Sahaj Samadhi Meditation is easy to learn and practice.

ART Excel (All Round Training In Excellence - 8 to 15 years) and **YOUNG ADULTS** (15 to 18 years) are fun workshops for children and teens, which also culture students in such values as acceptance of others, empathy, respect, trust and selfless giving. Students are challenged to go beyond their limited perspectives to consider the world at large with all its diversity. The true measure of success is a happy, healthy, well-adjusted child who is able to deal effectively with life's challenges - www.artexcel.info.

To learn more about the Art of Living Foundation and its programmes, visit www.artofliving.org.

Worldwide Art of Living Centers
The Art of Living Foundation is in more than 130 countries. For information about courses and programs near you, contact one of the centers below, or visit www.artofliving.org.

AFRICA
Hema & Rajaraman
Art of Living
P.O. Box 1213
Peba Close Plot 5612
Gaborone, Botswana
Tel. 26-735-2175
Aolbot@global.co.za

UNITED STATES
Art of Living Foundation
P.O. Box 50003
Santa Barbara, CA 93150
Tel. 805-564-1002
U.S. toll free: 877-399-1008
info@artofliving.org

CANADA
Art of Living Foundation
P.O. Box 170
13 Infinity Rd.
Saint-Mathieu-du-Parc
Quebec G0X 1N0
Canada
Tel. (819) 532-3328
artofliving.northamerica@sympatico.ca

JAKARTA
Yayasan Seni Kehidupan
Danau Indah, No. 2
Raya Block A-1
Sunter Podomora
Jakarta Hara 14350
Phone : 62-651 3123
Fax : 62-6513124

INDIA
Vyakti Vikas Kendra, India
No. 19, 39th A Cross, 11th Main
4th T Block, Jayanagar
Bangalore - 560041, India
Tel. 91-80-26645106
vvm@vsnl.com

GERMANY
Akademie Bad Antogast
Bad Antogast 1
77728 Oppenau
Germany
Tel. 49-7804-910-923

ART OF LIVING NZ
SIMIN WILLIAMS
PO BOX 997, GISBORNE, **NEW ZEALAND**
PH : (64) 06-868-8002, FAX : (64) 06-868-8042
<artofliving@xtra.co.nz>

The Art of Living

International Centre
Vyakti Vikas Kendra
19, 39th A Cross,
11th Main Road, 4th 'T' Block
Jayanagar, **Bangalore**-560 041.
Tel : (080) 26645106 Fax : 26635175
Email : vvkpress@bgl.vsnl.net.in

Campus
Ved Vignan Mahavidyapeeth
21st Km, Kanakapura Road
Udayapura
Bangalore South-560 082
Tel. (080) 28432274 Fax : 28432832
email : vvm@vsnl.com

www.artofliving.org

Some Centres of the Art of Living in India

D1 31, Side Portion
Model Town II
Delhi-110 009
Ph : 7432824, 4691055
Tel./Fax 6422221

V. K. Sood
Procolor Photographics
Sector 35C, S.C.O. 445-46
Chandigarh - 160 002
Ph : 0172 600412

114, Arjun Marg
DLF Phase - 1
Gurgaon - 122 006
Ph : 0124 364445

"Shabnam", Bharuwala
Clement Town
Dehradun - 248 002
Ph : 0135 640633

Bharath Bhushan Phull
Plot 121, Shopping Centre
Bakshi Nagar
Jammu - 180 001

Ashok Kumar Kothari
162, Barodia Basti
Kabir Marg
Jaipur - 302 016
Ph : 0141 203648

60, Mahanirban Road
'Pushpanjali', 2nd Floor
Calcutta - 700 029
Ph : 033 4631018

Shyam Bansal
Bhagwati Stores
Santdeep Building
Sevoke Road
Siligui - 734 401
Ph : 0353 431267

Prachi Parivahan
Gangwal Bhavan
Jain Gali Kedar Road
Guwahati - 781 001
Ph : 0361 522880

211 Adharshila Complex
Patna - 800 001
Ph : 0612 674264

Pravin Kumar
102, Sundaram Apts.
North Office Para
Doronda
Ranchi - 834 001
Ph : 0651 500969

784, Sadashiv Peth
Pune - 411 030
Ph : 0212 630541

A/3/A, Vidyadaini Co-op.
Hsg. Soc., Bhoomi Bldg.
C Wing, #1, Ground Floor
Andhere (E),
Mumbai - 400 099
Ph : 022 8203557

No. 33, Mangadu Swamu St.
Nungambakkam
Chennai - 600 034
Tel./Fax : 044 8239025

35/36, Shymal Row House
No. 3A, 132 Ft. Satellite Rd.
Near Someshware Temple
Ahmedabad - 380 009
Ph : 079 441480

1-Rajasthambh Society
Polo Ground South
Baroda - 390 001
Ph : 0265 423140, 370653

203, 4th Floor, Allaudin
Complex, Adj. Shopper's
Stop, Begumpet
Hyderabad - 500 016
Ph : 040 7768042

Allahabad : 0522-
545940, 541609